WHAT SNAKE IS THAT?

Introducing Australian Snakes

Gerry Swan and Steve Wilson

Published in Australia by Reed New Holland
an imprint of New Holland Publishers (Australia) Pty Ltd
Sydney • Auckland • London • Cape Town

Unit 1, 66 Gibbes Street Chatswood NSW 2067 Australia
218 Lake Road Northcote Auckland New Zealand
The Chandlery, Unit 11450 Westminster Bridge Road London SE1 7QY UK
Wembly Square First Floor Solan Street Gardens Cape Town 8001

Reprinted in 2009, 2012, 2014

National Library of Australia Cataloguing-in-Publication data:

Swan, Gerry.

What snake is that? / Gerry Swan.

9781877069574 (pbk.)

Snakes–Australia–Identification.

597.960994

Publisher: Fiona Schultz
Publishing manager: Lliane Clarke
Project editor: Diane Jardine
Design: Barbara Cowan
Cover design: Tania Gomes
Production manager: Linda Bottari
Printer: Everbest Printing Company, China

Front cover: Common Tree Snake (*Dendrelaphis punctulata*). Sydney, NSW. G. Swan
Back cover: Northern Tree Snake (*Dendrelaphis calligastra*). Iron Range, Qld. S. Wilson

… the venomous snake, of all the deadly creatures in nature, is slowest to resentment, the most reluctant to enter into a quarrel …

W.H. Hudson, *The Naturalist in La Plata*, 1892

contents

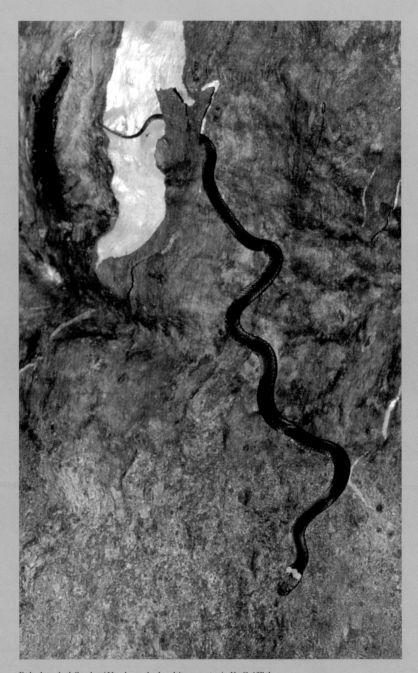

Pale-headed Snake (*Hoplocephalus bitorquatus*). K. Griffiths

Introduction

Infested with snakes

Snakes fascinate and repel but there is never a shortage of yarns about them. We endow them with a willingness to attack humans on sight and kill within minutes or seconds. When the conversation turns to snakes, the language is often loaded. We speak of 'snake-infested bushland', but the authors have yet to hear of a koala-infested eucalypt forest or a platypus-infested creek.

Harpers Magazine of March 1855 included the following: 'Of all animated life, the serpent at first sight, is the most repulsive, and yet, with the species, there is such a combination of the beautiful, the terrible, and the mysterious, that the beholder, in spite of himself, is attracted by their appearance.' Nothing much has changed in more than 150 years.

While enthusiasts fill rooms with heated snake-boxes and lavish great care and attention on their pet reptiles, there are horror-struck people who are unable to even glimpse a picture of a snake in a magazine without convulsively ripping the page. Snakes excite our imagination and hold us spellbound even if we fear them. Clearly, snakes polarise.

Yet snakes are extremely secretive animals that have mastered the art of remaining inconspicuous and unseen. They go to great lengths to avoid crossing paths and conflicting with humans. Most encounters are just a vanishing tail – ('thin … thinner … gone!') – or perhaps a large python slowly gliding across a track or curled up in the sun after a feast of possum, rat or bandicoot. Venomous snakes occur on the edges of all towns and cities, and occasionally they turn up as unwelcome visitors in our backyards. Their removal and liberation by approved fauna handlers has become a thriving business where once they were simply dispatched with a stick. Behind the scenes there is also a host of small burrowing and nocturnal snakes living among us, unseen until the household cat turns up after a night's hunting with a hapless specimen hanging from its jaws.

▲ Tiger Snake (*Notechis scutatus*). G. Swan

Where do snakes live?

There are almost 200 named Australian species of snakes in five families, living in areas as diverse as alpine meadows, tropical woodlands and rainforests, tidal mudflats, coral reefs, suburban gardens and even open oceans far from land. The hotspots are mainly northern tropical areas, where members of all families occur and large numbers of species partition the food resources, shelter sites and activity times. At the other end of the continent, cool temperate Tasmania is home to just three species in one family, but they are abundant on the island and often occur in high densities. Throughout most of mainland Australia, a given region may support anywhere from about five to more than 30 different species.

Peeling off their skins

Like all reptiles, snakes shed their skins as they grow. The outer layer consists of keratin, the same stuff that makes up our fingernails. This hard, dry covering provides the snake with some protection from abrasions and scratches, and helps retain moisture. But having such an inflexible veneer requires snakes to periodically shed their skins. This process is called *ecdysis* or, in everyday terms, shedding or sloughing.

Before sloughing the skin appears milky, as a fluid forms between the old outer layer and the new one beneath. The spectacles covering the lidless eyes are also shed, and these become noticeably opaque. At this time the snake cannot see, retires to a sheltered place and is irritable if disturbed. After several days the opaque appearance clears and shedding begins with the snake rubbing its snout against a fixed object. The old skin lifts back from the lips and over the head. As it catches against other objects, it is drawn back over the snake, peeling off inside-out like removing a tight stocking. Ideally sloughing is achieved in one piece. The sloughed skin contains little or no pigment and is largely colourless while the freshly moulted snake looks vibrant, clean and boldly patterned.

Snake scales overlap but on the sloughed skin they are stretched apart with the connective tissue clearly visible between each scale. This means the old skin is about 25 per cent longer than the live snake – always worth remembering if you find a sloughed skin in your garden and attempt to gauge the size of its owner!

Just after it has been shed the old skin is moist and soft, but it soon dries and hardens, becoming quite brittle. These skins are occasionally found tangled in grass, low shrubs or around rocks, but they break up quickly when exposed to the elements.

Added to their impermeable skin is the ability of snakes to convert soluble body wastes, primarily urea, into solid uric acid, passed as a white paste attached to the faeces and drying to a chalk-like substance. Their efficient water-conservation system is one of the factors enabling terrestrial snakes to successfully colonise arid areas. They drink when surface water is available, but many snakes gain most of their fluids metabolically from their prey. Provided they can find suitable humid shelter sites, snakes are important residents in deserts worldwide.

▲ Yellow-faced Whipsnake (*Demansia psammophis*). The opaque eye indicates the snake will soon shed its skin. J. Weigel

▲ Marsh Snake (*Hemiaspis signata*) shedding its skin. G. Swan

Sensing their world

It is commonly believed that snakes are deaf to airborne sounds, and only pick up vibrations through the ground surface. True, snakes have no external ears but they do have an inner ear mechanism, and airborne sounds are transmitted from the skin surface on the side of the skull, through the jaw muscle to the internal ear bone. Low frequency sounds are those most effectively picked up by this method.

Snakes more than compensate for the dubious quality of their hearing with their acute sense of smell and taste. The constantly flickering forked tongue is a highly developed organ that collects airborne and ground-borne particles and transfers them to a sophisticated chemical analysis plant called Jacobson's organ, located in the roof of the mouth. The snake can distinguish different particle loads on each lobe of the forked tongue, providing an accurate cue to direction. Whichever fork picks up the stronger scent is the one the snake will follow or avoid, depending on whether it senses prey, a potential mate or danger.

Because they lack eyelids, snakes view the world with a fixed stare that makes some people uncomfortable and probably underlies the myth of their ability to hypnotise prey. For snakes, vision ranges between acute and virtually non-existent. Those that are active during the day and hunt fast-moving prey usually have large eyes and keen eyesight, while many of the nocturnal snakes have small eyes, and a stronger reliance on chemo-reception. This goes against a common trend in mammals and birds, where nocturnal species tend to have larger eyes to compensate for the lower light. The Brown Tree Snake is exceptional in being nocturnal with very large eyes.

▲ Stephens' Banded Snake (*Hoplocephalus stephensii*). Snakes' forked tongues can determine the direction of chemical cues. K. Griffiths

▲ The Yellow-faced Whipsnake (*Demansia psammophis*) is a fast-moving diurnal snake that relies on acute vision. S. Wilson

▲ Brown Tree Snake (*Boiga irregularis*); unusual among nocturnal snakes in having large, light-sensitive eyes. G. Swan

Getting about

It is extraordinary that a group of animals completely devoid of functional limbs can get about so efficiently. Having about 400 vertebrae certainly helps with flexibility, but the key structures in the mobility of most snakes are the broad ventral scales spanning their bellies and the underlying musculature. These ventral scales are smoothly overlapping, each with a free hind edge. Combined with fluid, lateral undulating movements of the body, the scales catch on irregularities to propel the snake forward. A snake placed on a perfectly smooth surface goes through the motions but does not effectively get anywhere.

Depending on lifestyle, snakes have modified this basic plan to suit their needs. Tree snakes have an outer longitudinal keel along each side of the ventral scales, giving extra purchase that enables them to pick their way up brick walls and seemingly smooth tree trunks. Those venomous snakes that have embarked on a life at sea have made a compromise by reducing the size of their ventral scales in exchange for a laterally-compressed body for easy swimming. In addition, their tails are flattened and oar-shaped. The smooth, cylindrical blind snakes probably never had enlarged ventral scales. Their uniformly small, glossy scales slip easily through soil, aided by a short spur on the tail to push them along.

Large bulky snakes such as pythons sometimes employ a slow, straight-line way of moving called caterpillar locomotion. The head and forebody are stretched straight forward, the belly scales then gain a hold on the surface, and the snake advances by contracting the body muscles and dragging the rest of the body along.

▲ Dubois' Sea Snake (*Aipysurus duboisii*). North-east Qld. S. Swanson

▲ Tiger Snake (*Notechis scutatus*); moving. Devonport, Tas. S. Wilson

Snakes in soft sand or mud sometimes use a side-winding and side-pushing means of locomotion that propels the animal diagonally across the surface. The most famous and effective side-winders are the sand-inhabiting vipers of Northern America and Africa, but the White-bellied Mangrove Snake from northern Australian mud-flats sometimes moves by side-pushing. The head and neck are pushed against a surface and the body drawn forward in a loop. Once the rear end gains a grip, the body is again shifted forward.

Cold-blooded serpents

Many snakes have preferred operating temperatures similar to ours, so the popular term 'cold-blooded' is not accurate. They do not generate their own heat, however, and require an external source to raise their body temperatures. This is called *ectothermy*, and it confers both pluses and minuses in terms of efficiency and energy requirements. In a nutshell, snakes are sluggish and helpless in the absence of a heat source but they are cheap to run and can go for weeks, even months, without food. Our own internal heat generation, called *endothermy*, permits year-round activity in all climates but the fuel bill, in terms of nourishment and oxygen, is astronomical. We must eat daily to keep the furnace burning.

To gain heat, snakes bask in direct sunlight, absorb heat from a warmed surface or inhabit tropical areas where temperatures are uniformly high. By shuttling between sun and shade they can maintain relatively stable temperatures at an optimum level. Small wonder the tropics are rich in snakes.

In cool environments, snakes must carefully select basking sites, and to maximise heat gain and storage they are often dark coloured and thick bodied. They may also be forced to enter a period of hibernation or torpor for at least part of the year when daytime temperatures are too low for normal daily activities. At this time they can live off accumulated body fat, and remain inactive within the hibernation site. Occasionally they emerge to bask in the middle of a warm winter day.

What's for dinner?

Snakes are carnivorous. There are no vegetarians. In many parts of the world they dine on a varied menu ranging from antelopes to slugs and snails, centipedes and insects, even newly-moulted freshwater crayfish.

Australian snakes appear to be fussy eaters. With few exceptions, they prey only on vertebrates. Some also take bird or reptile eggs. Many species feed on just one group of animals – there are mammal, frog and lizard specialists – while others are opportunists that take a range of vertebrates. Some shift their diets as they grow. For example, young pythons begin feeding on skinks, usually graduating later to larger furred prey. By far the favourite food item for Australian snakes is lizards.

As a rule, Australian snakes avoid eating invertebrates. Notable exceptions are the insectivorous blind snakes and the crab-eating White-bellied Mangrove Snake. Live prey is preferred, though there are a few records of snakes eating road-killed animals. There are even verified accounts of snakes swallowing the china eggs used to induce laying in poultry. Presumably their chemo-receptors informed them that these inedible items were loaded with 'essence of chook'.

Snakes cannot dismember their food. They must select items they can swallow whole. For swift, thin snakes like whipsnakes, capturing and devouring a slender-bodied skink is a relatively simple process. But some snakes are famous for consuming enormous meals, and thanks to loosely articulated skulls, elastic skin and extendable openings to their tracheas, they can dispatch animals with girths much greater than their own.

▲ Marsh Snake (*Hemiaspis signata*); eating a lizard. S. Wilson

While the brain is safely encased in bone, all other elements of the skull are extremely flexible. The lower jaw is not joined at the front, but linked by very elastic tissue. It can also drop down at the back and stretch sideways, and both sides of the upper and lower jaws are capable of independent movement. This means that a snake has a prodigious gape and the ability to work each side of its jaw forward separately. It can literally 'walk' the mouth over its prey, using sharp, backward-curved teeth to anchor and pull.

With a distended face full of food, one wonders how the snake can breathe. Close examination of a feeding snake reveals the circular opening of its trachea protruding forward below the prey. This breathing tube, ribbed with cartilage to prevent crushing or compression, is extendable so the snake can breathe while it eats.

These are all essential modifications if a large python is to spend several hours ingesting a whole wallaby. Having done so, and found a sheltered sunny place to coil its bloated body and digest its meal, the snake can go for many months without eating. For large snakes, it is more efficient to catch and eat one hefty meal rather than spend a lot of effort taking many smaller animals.

Venom

Snake venom has three main functions. It kills or incapacitates prey, aids digestion by breaking down tissue, and acts as a deterrent to possible predators. Venom is modified saliva containing a mix of proteins and enzymes that originally evolved to play a role in faster digestion. The evolution of a more potent brew, combined with increasingly efficient means of storing and delivering it, has occurred many times among snakes, leading to venomous species in several families.

Aquatic snakes of the family Homalopsidae, and some members of the family Colubridae, including Australia's Brown Tree Snake, have fangs situated at the rear of the mouth. However, most Australian venomous snakes, including all medically significant species, belong to the family Elapidae, characterised by having relatively short, fixed fangs at the front of the mouth.

The venom is stored in glands situated behind the eyes and carried to the front of the head where it enters a duct or groove in the fangs and travels down to the tip. A snake can control the amount of venom administered. Sometimes an extremely lucky snake-bite victim may receive none. In captive situations a snake that is normally offered dead prey may miss its mark and bite the hand that feeds it, but deliver no venom.

Venom contains a number of active components. Their presence and complexity differ between snakes but are similar in closely related species. For this reason, anti-venoms are structured to target broad venom groups rather than tailored for particular snake species.

Venoms affect the body in a number of ways. The neurotoxins disrupt transmission of information by the nervous system, often resulting in paralysis of the diaphragm and suffocation. The myotoxins break down muscle tissue, and a follow-on effect of severe muscle destruction may be kidney failure. This venom component has obvious advantages in prey digestion. Haemotoxins affect the blood and interfere with clotting properties. Some haemotoxins are coagulants, which enhance the formation of clots, while others are anti-coagulants, which prevent clotting and cause bleeding and haemorrhages. Haemotoxins can also contain components that destroy red blood cells.

Classifying snakes

This book is an introduction to those fascinating and misunderstood reptiles, the snakes. It covers all the groups of Australian snakes but does not attempt to portray all of the species. That is the role of a field guide or other identification book, and such publications are only effective if they are fully comprehensive for a region, a state or the country. Where identification features are of particular interest they are provided, and key pointers offer hints to general diagnostic aspects.

Scientists classify related species of snakes together in genera. Members of a genus have similar features and share a common ancestor. It is traditional in any systematic treatment to list each genus and species in alphabetical order within their respective families, but that approach has not been strictly followed here.

People are generally more interested in whether a snake is harmful or what unusual habits it has, so within each family the genera are grouped together on the basis of how we relate to them, their ecology or other behavioural traits.

According to the traditional alphabetic approach, two of our most lethal genera, the death adders (*Acanthophis*) and the taipans (*Oxyuranus*), appear near opposing ends of the diverse elapid family. In this book they are drawn together with other famous names, including the copperheads, brown, tiger and black snakes, under one banner. They are the snakes we generally regard as dangerous.

Snakes that are swift, slender, keen-eyed and hunt for lizards by day share important hunting strategies and general appearance, as do the suite of small nocturnal snakes that seize their lizard quarry at night while it sleeps. Likewise, common features of small snakes that burrow through the soil are strikingly banded or ringed bodies and shovel-shaped heads. These snakes all appear in pigeon-holes reflecting their similar lifestyles.

Of course, some species could easily be allotted to more than one category. The Eastern Small-eyed Snake (*Cryptophis nigrescens*) appears with its cousins that are all nocturnal hunters preying mainly on lizards, and the three broad-headed snakes (*Hoplocephalus*) form a natural group because of their unusual climbing habits. Yet these snakes all inflict bites that can be considered serious. The authors have chosen to place these snakes in groups that broadly reflect their ecology, while at the same time adding comments that bites are likely to pose problems.

Most snakes have both scientific and common names, but the common names vary in their application. For example, in south-eastern Australia the Yellow-bellied Black Snake is likely to be one of the copperheads but in north-eastern Australia the name is used for some colour variants of the harmless Common Tree Snake. Such a mix-up could potentially have dire consequences.

Some snakes have no common name and can only be labelled with their scientific names. Whether we like it or not, scientific names are our primary labels for these animals. Scientific names are applied throughout this book, and where common names are in use, they have been employed as well. Readers seeking information on particular snakes will do better to search them out using the thorough index rather than hunting for them alphabetically in the body of the book.

Coastal Carpet Python (*Morelia spilota mcdowelli*); after eating. S. Wilson

The underground movement: the blind snakes

Thanks to their blunt heads and tails, glossy cylindrical bodies and small rudimentary eyes set below smooth head scales, the more than 40 different species of Australian blind snakes are often mistaken for worms. Not surprisingly, these secretive burrowing snakes are often called worm snakes. At first glance it can even be difficult to tell which end is which.

All Australian blind snakes are in the genus *Ramphotyphlops*. Blind snakes are considered to be primitive snakes because, within their outwardly similar bodies, there lies a structure linking them to an ancient time when snakes and lizards parted company to wriggle and walk their separate ways. Blind snakes have a pelvis. It is no longer functional and there are no limbs attached but it provides evidence of a limbed ancestry. More modern snakes – virtually all other groups, with the notable exceptions of pythons and boas – have completely done away with this vestige.

Blind snakes occur throughout Australia, except in Tasmania and far south-eastern Victoria, and live in most habitats from moist forests to sandy deserts. These snakes spend virtually all their lives below ground in the cavities of ant and termite nests and in soil under rocks and logs. One extremely thin, thread-like species may only occur in deep subterranean cavities. It is known from a single individual removed from a bore-casing during drilling operations. Interestingly, there have been several reports of blind snakes found 2 metres or higher under the loose bark of dead standing trees, and even a record of a blind snake climbing a sapling. Aggregations of blind snakes, including both adults and juveniles, have been uncovered but the reason they have come together remains unclear.

Many blind snake species are so superficially alike that they cannot be reliably identified in the field. Others differ in colour, head-shape and size. They range from pink to almost black, and some have contrastingly darker heads and/or tails. The belly is usually lighter than the top but, depending on species, the colours may merge gradually or change abruptly along a jagged interface. Snout-shapes vary from smoothly rounded to tri-lobed and some are acutely beaked, possibly reflecting different preferred soil types or favoured shelter sites. The smallest blind snakes are only 17 centimetres long and scarcely thicker than a match while the largest, looking like fat, elongated sausages, are known to reach 75 centimetres.

All except a poorly-known species from central Queensland have a small, sharp spur on the rounded tail tip, used to anchor the snake as it pushes its head through the soil. When the snake is handled, a slight prick can sometimes be felt from this spine as the animal struggles. This may be mistaken for a sting. They are completely harmless and non-venomous. It would be impossible for a blind snake to bite, even if it tried, given the position of the tiny mouth, set below the head and well back from the snout.

It is extremely unlikely that the greatly reduced eyes can form any meaningful images but they are acutely sensitive to

▲ Robust Blind Snake (*Ramphotyphlops ligatus*). Southwood, Qld. S. Wilson

▲ Cooloola Blind Snake (*Ramphotyphlops silvia*). Fraser Island, Qld. S. Wilson

▼ Beaked Blind Snake (*Ramphotyphlops grypus*). Port Hedland area, WA. R. Browne-Cooper

light. If these snakes are unearthed by day, they immediately attempt to burrow back into darkness. This means they must rely entirely on chemical markers to locate food and mates.

Blind snakes are the only fully insectivorous Australian snakes, and it appears they eat termites and the larvae and pupae of ants. Protected by a smooth body and tough, bite-proof scales, they can inhabit the galleries of an ant nest and consume their prey largely immune to attack. It is possible that they also acquire the appropriate scent of their hosts, so many ants may not recognise them as the unwanted predatory lodgers that they really are. The larger, more robust species can even take on bulldog ant nests with impunity, but the smaller, more slender species probably select smaller ants. Actual feeding has rarely been witnessed, but the few observations reveal how the soft bodies of their prey are seized in their small mouths and swallowed with surprising haste.

Blind snakes are non-venomous and inoffensive, so must rely on other defences. When handled they wriggle and squirm continuously and many emit a foul-smelling substance from glands in the cloaca. It is often necessary, after removing a blind snake from a wet road at night, to stop at puddles several times in an attempt to wash the stuff off. While this obviously deters some predators, one small venomous snake, the Bandy-bandy, feeds on blind snakes exclusively. Based on knowledge about a small number of species, all are presumed to be egg-layers, with clutch sizes ranging from one to 34.

Australia's only introduced snake is a blind snake. **The Flower Pot Snake** (*Ramphotyphlops braminus*) arrived among soil in pot plants and other containers. It was first recorded here in the 1960s and has since spread to towns and cities across

▲ Blackish Blind Snake (*Ramphotyphlops nigrescens*); tail showing spine. Sydney, NSW. G. Swan

▲ Woodland Blind Snake (*Ramphotyphlops proximus*); blind snakes' eyes are protected under smooth, clean scales. Wallumbillah, Qld. S. Wilson

▲ Blind snake eating ant larvae and pupae. J. Weigel

northern Australia. It has also been accidentally transported to many other tropical areas of the world. The snake is so tiny it is an easy stowaway, but it is a particularly successful disperser because of the way it reproduces. The populations consist only of females, who lay viable eggs with no input from any male. They produce clones, and just one individual is all that is required to arrive at a locality and found a whole new population.

Because of their secretive burrowing habits, most species in this unusual family of snakes are poorly known. They are difficult to find, and normally encountered opportunistically when crossing roads at night. Even the keenest herpetologist has little chance of identifying many species in the field and we are privy to rare glimpses of any natural behaviour. Apart from wriggling in the hand, emitting their repellant fluids and burrowing from the light, their lives are largely a mystery. Nearly 10 per cent of Australian species are known from fewer than half a dozen individuals and several from single specimens. It is highly likely that many more await discovery. Clearly, there is much more to blind snakes than meets the eye!

Telltale signs

→ Shiny, cylindrical worm-like bodies with a blunt head and tail.
→ The eyes are represented by two small dark spots.
→ The tip of the tail has a short conical spine.
→ The mouth is located under the jaw and back from the snout.

▲ Flower Pot Snake (*Ramphotyphlops braminus*). Townsville, Qld. S. Wilson

Baggy fish-eaters: the file snakes

▲ Arafura File Snake (*Acrochordus arafurae*). Lawn Hill, Qld. S Wilson

The two highly specialised, fully aquatic file snakes (*Acrochordus*) occur in waters of tropical northern Australia and a third is confined to South-east Asia. The Arafura File Snake (*A. arafurae*) inhabits fresh water, while the Little File Snake (*A. granulatus*) is found in coastal marine and estuarine habitats, occasionally entering fresh water. These stout-bodied snakes have loose, baggy skin covered by numerous very small rasp-like scales. The head is short and blunt with small eyes and the nostrils are placed well forward, allowing the snake to breathe in the water with just the tip of the snout exposed. Their unusual shape and texture has led to them being given several inelegant names,

including wart snakes and elephant's trunk snakes. Both are non-venomous.

It seems that these exclusive fish-eaters live life in the slow lane. They are lethargic snakes that lie in ambush among roots and under overhangs, or forage slowly by exploring cavities and other potential retreats. File snakes can eat very large prey, aided by their loosely articulated skulls and elastic skin. They capture their prey with a rapid strike, and sometimes even seize fish directly in their coils. While large fish are held in the snakes' coils, small fish are grasped and immediately swallowed alive.

The pointed scales probably help in holding slippery fish, but they also sprout fine hair-like sense organs that are likely to serve a vital tactile function. Vision is often poor in turbid water, and file snakes have been observed to ignore fish that swim past their heads, but attempt to catch them if they contact the snake.

When swimming, file snakes flatten their bodies laterally and move with graceful, fluid undulations. They are able to stay totally submerged for over two hours. However, on land these baggy-skinned snakes are much less refined, with all the charm and agility of a wet sock full of porridge. They are largely helpless out of the water but can move clumsily over short distances.

The 2 metre **Arafura File Snake** is brown to olive, with blackish reticulations forming a series of blotches along the body. It is found in freshwater lagoons, rivers and floodplains bordering the Arafura Sea, including southern New Guinea and the Gulf of Carpentaria drainage systems. During the dry season, when water has contracted to pools and rivers, huge numbers become concentrated in relatively small areas. With wet season flooding they disperse widely through the water channels and across the floodplains. Arafura File Snakes feed mainly in the wet season and are dependent upon a good supply of fish to put on enough condition for breeding. Females produce 11–25 live young, but only

▲ Arafura File Snake (*Acrochordus arafurae*). The position of the nostrils allows the snake to breathe in the water without exposing its whole head. Lawn Hill, Qld. S. Wilson

▲ Arafura File Snake (*Acrochordus arafurae*); swimming. Gregory River, Qld. J. Cann

a small number of females reproduce each year. The young are born between February and April after a gestation period of about 6 months.

These snakes are mainly active at night. During the day they hide among submerged vegetation and under overhanging riverbanks or logs. They have long been a prized food for Aboriginal people, with the women traditionally gathering them. They are captured by wading into the water and feeling under banks and logs to locate the snakes by touch, then dispatched with a bite behind the head, and tossed up onto the bank.

The 1.5 metre **Little File Snake** is marked with simple dark and pale bands. This widespread species includes northern Australia as part of a broader distribution extending from the Solomon Islands to India. It is usually found in mud flats, mangrove swamps and reef flats. It has also been reported in the open sea at depths up to 20 metres. This file snake appears to be active both during the day and at night, and hides by burying into soft substrate, sheltering in burrows under debris and among mangrove roots. Females produce 1–12 live young in April–May after a gestation period of 6–8 months.

Telltale signs

→ Very small rough scales.

→ Baggy body when out of water.

→ Small eyes on top of head.

→ Totally aquatic.

▲ Little File Snake (*Acrochordus granulatus*). Darwin, NT. S. Swanson

A mixed bunch: the colubrids

▲ Brown Tree Snake (*Boiga irregularis*). It has a wide gape and rapid strike. Manning Creek, WA. S. Wilson

The family Colubridae includes both non-venomous and venomous species. Those with venom have grooved fangs located at the rear of the mouth. Colubrids have large, symmetrically arranged scales on top of the head and their broad ventral scales extend fully across the belly.

Colubridae is an extraordinarily successful group of snakes, encompassing a suite of burrowing, climbing, aquatic and terrestrial species. There are about 1600 different kinds, comprising about half of the world's snake species. Colubrids are found virtually anywhere on Earth where snakes are capable of surviving. In terms of species diversity, they generally outnumber all other families of snakes wherever they occur. The only exception is Australia, where isolation appears to have kept their advance at bay.

Australia's rich and complex snake fauna includes only a token number of colubrid species, while the endemic lineage of front-fanged venomous elapid snakes has evolved, diversified and radiated to fill many of the niches traditionally exploited elsewhere by colubrids.

The significance of Australia's bias away from colubrids is best appreciated when compared to a few other parts of the world. The island of Borneo in South-east Asia has approximately 154 species of snakes, including at least 96 colubrids. Of about 130 species of snakes in southern Africa, around 58 are colubrids, while the United States and Canada have about 115 snake species, of which 92 are colubrids. Australia is home to 197 described species of snakes, but just 6 are colubrids.

▲ Brown Tree Snake (*Boiga irregularis*); Night Tiger colour form. Manning Creek, WA. S. Wilson

Colubrids are relatively recent arrivals to Australia, and none of them are endemic to Australia – all species are shared at least with New Guinea. Australian colubrids are absent from the deserts and temperate regions. They are largely confined to the tropics, extending down the east coast to the Sydney area. Their specialty appears to be niches that Australian elapid snakes have been less inclined to exploit – trees, rock faces and moist areas adjacent to fresh water. Within that relatively limited scope colubrids are abundant in the areas they occupy. They account for a large proportion of snake encounters in many parts of northern and eastern Australia, and a few species have adapted extremely well to modified human environments.

Out on a limb: the tree snakes

A slender, supple body and keen vision are among the key ingredients allowing limbless animals to climb skilfully. Their ability to gain purchase on small irregularities allows them to scale seemingly smooth tree trunks and sheer brick walls. Because of their light weight they can navigate thin branches and bridge gaps between foliage. They also have to rely strongly on eyesight when hunting, as chemical trails laid by potential prey are often not as easily followed as they are on land. The two genera of tree snakes in Australia include three species that are superbly adapted for life off the ground.

The **Brown Tree Snake** or **Night Tiger** (*Boiga irregularis*) is weakly venomous with fangs set at the rear of the mouth. It has large prominent eyes and cat-like vertical pupils, a bulbous head and a very narrow neck. It can grow to 2 metres long. Two very distinct regional colour forms exist. On the east coast of New South Wales and Queensland the Brown Tree Snake is a reddish brown above with narrow, dark bands that are irregular and sometimes obscure. Underneath it is orange to salmon pink. Across northern Australia the Night Tiger variant is cream with prominent reddish brown bands

▲ Brown Tree Snake (*Boiga irregularis*); east coast colour form. Mount Glorious, Qld. S. Wilson

This nocturnal snake occurs in a variety of habitats from woodlands to rainforest, rock outcrops and escarpments. It frequently occupies caves, often festooning its shed skins over walls and ceilings. It is a slow and deliberate climber and preys upon birds, small mammals and lizards. Eggs are also taken. Much of its prey is captured while they are asleep. It is not uncommon for this agile climber to scale walls and rafters to access hanging bird-cages where, having consumed the occupants, it remains trapped for the horrified owners to discover in the morning.

When confronted the Brown Tree Snake raises its forebody to form tight S-shaped loops. If provoked it does not hesitate to strike. Normally the venom has little or no effect on humans and is not regarded as dangerous.

While native to Australia, Melanesia and parts of South-east Asia, this snake has achieved considerable notoriety after having been introduced accidentally onto the Pacific island of Guam during World War II. It continues to cause severe problems, including an explosive population growth, the extinction of local bird species and frequent power outages as it shortcircuits wiring and hides in fuse-boxes.

Telltale signs

→ Slender with large head and prominent eyes with vertical pupils.

→ Nocturnal.

→ Distinctive defensive pose.

▲ Common Tree Snake (*Dendrelaphis punctulata*); yellow northern colour form. Lawn Hill, Qld. S. Wilson

Common Tree Snake (*Dendrelaphis punctulata*). Sydney, NSW. G. Swan

The Common Tree Snake (*Dendrelaphis punctulata*) and the Northern Tree Snake (*D. calligastra*) are non-venomous. Both have large eyes with round pupils and acute vision, and are active during the day. At any sign of movement, whether from perceived threat or prey, they raise their heads and sway from side to side, gaining an accurate assessment of distance. They are swift, skilled climbers, moving through foliage with fluid grace. They also frequently forage on the ground. Both species prey on frogs, tadpoles and lizards. When threatened they flatten the throat and body to display paler skin between the scales. They are generally reluctant to bite but give off an unpleasant odour from anal glands if handled.

▲ Common Tree Snake (*Dendrelaphis punctulata*); yellow and black colour form. Ross River, Qld. S. Wilson

▲ Northern Tree Snake (*Dendrelaphis calligastra*).
Iron Range, Qld. S. Wilson

▶ Common Tree Snake (*Dendrelaphis punctulata*);
in defensive pose. Sydney, NSW. G. Swan

The **Northern Tree Snake**, from far north-eastern Queensland is extremely thin and grows to just over 1 metre. It is brown to olive with a distinctive black stripe from the snout through the eye and onto the forebody. This is a very wary snake that is difficult to approach. It is usually seen (albeit very briefly) in sunny areas along edges of rainforests and vine thickets.

The 1.5 metre **Common Tree Snake** is also known as the Green Tree Snake, but considering this is one of Australia's most variable species that name seems both inadequate and misleading. Depending on region and individual variation, snakes range from olive green, bluish green or blue in eastern Australia, to yellow with a bluish head and neck across northern Australia, and black in mid-eastern Queensland. Many specimens are yellow underneath, giving rise to the mythical 'Yellow-bellied Black Snake'. It extends from the Sydney area, along the east coast and across northern Australia, occurring in woodlands, rainforest and even suburban gardens. In drier parts of its range it is often associated with thick vegetation along watercourses.

Telltale signs

→ Large eyes with round pupils.
→ Unpleasant smell if handled.
→ Pale skin visible between scales when alarmed.
→ Angular keel along each side of belly.

The non-venomous water snakes

Three species of non-venomous snakes are often associated with water. One, the **Slate-brown Snake** (*Stegonotus parvus*), is widespread in New Guinea but is only known in Australia from Murray Island in far north-eastern Torres Strait. The remainder are widespread tropical species and, although they are not aquatic, are found near water where they prey largely on frogs and lizards. All are egg-layers.

The 1.3 metre **Slatey-grey Snake** (*Stegonotus cucullatus*) is a uniform dark brown to almost black with smooth, highly polished scales. When viewed from some angles it appears an iridescent purple. It is usually associated with waterways or lagoons but also occurs in nearby rainforest and woodlands from Cape York Peninsula to northern regions of the Northern Territory. This crepuscular to

▲ Slatey-grey Snake (*Stegonotus cucullatus*). Darwin, NT. S Wilson

nocturnal snake preys upon frogs, lizards, fish, and also on the eggs of other reptiles. There are enlarged broad rear teeth in the upper jaw that may be used to slit these eggs as they are being swallowed. Anyone dealing with this species will quickly realise it has a nasty disposition. It bites repeatedly when provoked, and releases an unpleasant odour if handled.

The **Keelback** or **Freshwater Snake** (*Tropidonophis mairii*) is so named because of the distinctive raised longitudinal ridge or keel on each scale along the back and sides, aligning to form a series of prominent ridges down the body. This often leads to confusion with the highly venomous Rough-scaled Snake (see page 89). The Keelback comes in a wide range of colours from grey, olive or yellow to reddish brown, with or

Telltale signs

→ Shiny with a uniform colouration.
→ Active early evening and at night.
→ May release an unpleasant odour if handled.

▲ Slatey-grey Snake (*Stegonotus cucullatus*). Locality unknown. K. Griffiths

▲ Keelback (*Tropidonophis mairii*); eating a cane toad. Kurwongbah, Qld. S. Wilson

without narrow dark bands, spots or variegations. It can grow to more than 90 centimetres, though most individuals are 50–75 centimetres.

This snake frequents well-watered habitats from the Northern Rivers region of New South Wales, along eastern Queensland and across northern Australia. It is active by night and day, depending on temperature. The Keelback feeds on tadpoles, frogs, fish and lizards. It is Australia's sole representative of a worldwide group of colubrid snakes called natricines. These snakes prey heavily on frogs and toads and from this ancestry the Keelback appears to have inherited a degree of tolerance to toad poisons. Following the disastrous introduction of the highly poisonous Cane Toad into Australia in 1935, native predators crashed. Yet it was no quantum leap for the Keelback to include the new arrival in its diet. Attempts to ingest large toads can be fatal, but it is among the few native animals able to prey on the tadpoles and smaller individuals.

This is one of the few snakes able to break off the tail if handled roughly, a trait more usually associated with lizards, but in the case of the Keelback the tail does not regrow. It can also give off an unpleasant odour from anal glands if handled roughly.

The Keelback's similarity to the dangerously venomous Rough-scaled Snake demonstrates the importance of leaving snakes well alone unless absolutely necessary. Certainly no snake should be handled until its identity is established.

Telltale signs

→ Non-shiny, rough scales.

→ Can lose tail.

→ May release an unpleasant odour if handled.

→ Two rows of scales under tail.

▲ Keelback (*Tropidonophis mairii*). Wynnum, Qld. S. Wilson

▲ Keelback (*Tropidonophis mairii*). Thornton Peak, Qld. G. Swan

In shallow water and mud: the homalopsid snakes

It is small wonder that Australia's tropical rear-fanged water snakes are not often encountered. Searching for snakes in rainforests, alpine meadows or along outback highways is one thing, but patrolling soupy mud and tepid shallow water in a northern mangrove swamp is quite another. Few environments are as physically unpleasant for humans, with stifling humidity, rank smells, the constant whine of biting insects plus a very real risk of being eaten by a crocodile. Naturalists seldom venture into these areas. At best, we tinker nervously around the edges.

Though not often seen, snakes of the family Homalopsidae are an extremely successful group that comprise a significant proportion of the biomass in the areas they inhabit. This means they can be extremely abundant, so in the right location they can be seen not just in ones and twos, but by the dozen.

There are four species of aquatic homalopsid snakes in Australia, each in a different genus. Three are adapted to live in coastal and estuarine mangrove swamps and mud flats, and one inhabits freshwater rivers and streams. They are equipped with valvular nostrils, placed on the top of the snout to enable them to breathe from below the surface without exposing too much of the head. They differ from the marine elapids or true sea snakes in having a round tail rather than a laterally flattened, paddle-shaped tail. All are venomous, with grooved fangs situated at the back of the mouth, but none are regarded as dangerous to humans.

The marine homalopsids thrive in shallow water and mud. They probably follow rising and falling tides, enabling them to continually occupy their preferred water depth. They shelter in mangrove roots and crustacean burrows. Most prey exclusively on fish, but one highly specialised species takes only crustaceans.

Homalopsids are primarily nocturnal, though they can be seen active by day, particularly during overcast, drizzly weather. Most, probably all, species, extend from northern Australia to southern New Guinea, and one reaches South Asia. All are live-bearers.

The **Australian Bockadam** (*Cerberus australis*) is a distinctive 60-centimetre snake with small, protrusive, upward-directed eyes and keeled body scales. Two colour forms occur. Most are grey-brown with narrow dark bands, but occasional individuals are brick red. The Bockadam occurs in mangrove-lined tidal watercourses and estuaries where it feeds on fish, particularly mud skippers, which it actively searches out in holes and crevices. It has been recorded as staying submerged for almost 1 hour. It is pugnacious if provoked, flattening the body, striking repeatedly and emitting a foul-smelling odour from anal glands.

Telltale signs

► Found in salt or brackish water.
► Keeled scales.
► Protrusive, upwardly directed eyes with vertically elliptic pupils.

▲ Australian Bockadam (*Cerberus australis*); grey colour form. Buffalo Creek, Darwin, NT. S. Wilson

▲ Australian Bockadam (*Cerberus australis*); red colour form. Rapid Creek, NT. S. Swanson

▲ Macleay's Water Snake (*Enhydris polylepis*). Anniversary Creek, NT. B. Maryan

Macleay's Water Snake (*Enhydris polylepis*) grows to about 87 centimetres. It has a long head, small, upwardly directed eyes and smooth, highly polished scales. It is brown, olive or grey with or without stripes or bands, and usually with a dark stripe along the belly and tail. This is Australia's only exclusively freshwater homalopsid, living in creeks, swamps and lagoons from northern Queensland to the north of the Northern Territory. It shelters among aquatic vegetation, roots or debris and employs both ambush and active searching to locate prey such as tadpoles, frogs and fish. Scavenging is rarely reported among snakes, but is known in several homalopsid species overseas.

Telltale signs

→ Found in fresh water.

→ Smooth, very glossy scales.

→ Long head and upwardly directed eyes with vertically elliptic pupils.

The **White-bellied Mangrove Snake** (*Fordonia leucobalia*) is an extremely variable species, ranging from black through brown to reddish brown and cream, with or without pale blotches, spots or bands. This 90-centimetre snake has a broad head, short rounded snout, small eyes with round pupils and smooth polished glossy scales. It occurs in mangrove-lined channels and mud flats where it shelters in crab-holes. It is unique among Australian snakes, both in its diet and means of dealing with prey. The particularly robust, dagger-like fangs are designed to puncture the exoskeletons of crabs and mud lobsters. It usually takes small crustaceans and swallows them whole, but if prey is too large it can bite off legs and claws before consuming the body. It is the most widespread homalopsid snake, extending from northern Australia to Bangladesh.

Telltale signs

→ Found in salt or brackish water.

→ Smooth, glossy scales.

→ Broad head and small eyes with round pupils.

▲ White-bellied Mangrove Snake (*Fordonia leucobalia*). Wyndham, WA. S. Wilson

Richardson's Mangrove Snake (*Myron richardsonii*) is the smallest homalopsid snake, reaching only 43 centimetres. It is grey, olive to olive brown, with many narrow, irregular dark bands, a long narrow head, small upwardly directed eyes and weakly keeled scales. It occurs in mangrove-lined creeks, estuaries and mud flats, where it shelters among mangrove roots, in burrows and can even vanish into liquid mud when pursued. At night it hunts in the shallows for fish, particularly gobies, which it subdues with constriction. It has long anterior teeth, perhaps an adaptation for grasping slimy prey.

▲ Richardson's Mangrove Snake (*Myron richardsonii*). Darwin, NT. S. Swanson

Telltale signs

→ Found in salt or brackish water.

→ Weakly keeled scales.

→ Long head and upwardly directed eyes with vertically elliptic pupils.

Putting on the squeeze: the pythons

▲ Coastal Carpet Python (*Morelia spilota mcdowelli*); incubating eggs. Burpengary, Qld. S Wilson

The word 'python' conjures up images of immense size – giant snakes. The idea is well founded, for the family includes enormous reptiles such as the Reticulated Python (*Python reticulatus*) of South-east Asia, which has been reliably measured at nearly 10 metres long. It preys on mammals the size of deer, and sometimes even humans. The largest known Australian python, the Australian Scrub Python (*Morelia kinghorni*) reaches about 6 metres while the diminutive Anthill Python (*Antaresia perthensis*) is the world's smallest species at a mere 60 centimetres. Australia is home to 13 species, representing about half the world's pythons.

Most pythons are tropical species, and a single northern location may support up to six different kinds. Numbers drop sharply in temperate areas. Carpet and Diamond Pythons, both races of one highly variable and versatile species, extend south as far as eastern Victoria and the south-west of Western Australia.

Pythons are non-venomous, generally sedentary snakes that live life in the slow lane. They prefer to hunt by ambush rather than by active foraging, sometimes lying in wait for days beside an animal trail. Most species are equipped with heat-sensitive pits along the lips, enabling them to detect warm-blooded animals via infra-red heat. Because the heat-sensory mechanisms are set within pits, infra-red heat casts shadows as it enters. This provides the python with an accurate direction-seeking capacity, sensitive to mere fractions of a degree Celsius. When combined with the forked tongue, pythons are armed with a sophisticated thermal and chemical map of their surroundings.

Pythons strike rapidly and have a formidable array of long, sharp, backward-curved teeth. Prey is held fast and quickly enveloped in tight coils to constrict and suffocate. They are famous for their ability to consume huge prey items, aided by very loosely articulated skulls. They also have a higher number of body scale rows than most snakes. Their smaller and more numerous scales permit much greater elasticity to the skin.

Having spent up to several hours consuming a wallaby, possum or other large prey, a bloated python seeks a warm sheltered site to digest its meal. A substantial feed may last the snake many months or even a year.

All pythons are egg-layers and females exhibit a degree of maternal care that is rare in snakes. The freshly laid eggs are clumped together into a single cluster and the female coils around them to guard them. She leaves the eggs for short periods to bask in the sun, returning to the nest to transfer the heat. If temperatures drop too far the brooding female can actually shiver, generating heat to raise her body temperature and keep the eggs warm. Once they hatch, the young are on their own to disperse and look after themselves.

Buried within the body of all pythons is a vestigial pelvis, a legacy of their limbed ancestry. They also reveal external remnants of hind limbs in the form of a small spur either side of the vent. Courting males use these spurs to stimulate receptive mates, raking them over the back half of the female's body.

Pythons are often quite attractive, and are usually motionless when encountered – but never underestimate them. The hunting strategy they have evolved, lying coiled and still for lengthy periods ready to unleash an extremely swift, accurate strike at short

▲ Rough-scaled Python (*Morelia carinata*); head. Captive bred. B. Maryan

▲ Coastal Carpet Python (*Morelia spilota mcdowelli*); striking with long, sharp teeth clearly visible. West End, Qld. S. Wilson

◀ Top End Carpet Python (*Morelia spilota variegata*); head showing heat pits. Darwin district, NT. S Wilson

notice, holds them in good stead for defence. They are non-venomous snakes, but a bite from a large python can be painful and is usually very bloody. They also commonly dislodge one or more of their slender sharp teeth into the wound, so there is a risk of infection.

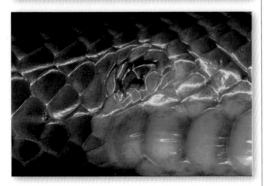

▲ Water Python (*Liasis mackloti*). The cloacal spurs are vestigal hind limbs. Cairns, Qld. S. Wilson

Telltale signs

- → Slow moving with robust bodies.
- → Vestiges of hindlimbs in the form of a pelvic spur on each side of the vent.
- → Sharp recurved teeth.
- → Heat-sensitive pits in the scales of the lower lips (except the Black-headed Python and Woma).

Pygmies and Children's: the smallest pythons

▲ Pygmy Python (*Antaresia perthensis*). Waldburg Stn, WA. S. Wilson

The four pythons in the genus *Antaresia* rarely reach 1 metre. Included is the world's smallest python, which only grows to about 60 centimetres. They are sometimes known collectively as Children's Pythons. The name is not derived from children, but because the first species described was named after a Mr J. Children at the British Museum. That said, they are generally docile snakes that are popular with reptile keepers, particularly beginners, because of their small size and quiet temperament. They are distributed across the northern two-thirds of Australia, mainly in dry habitats.

The **Pygmy Python** or **Anthill Python** (*Antaresia perthensis*) is the world's smallest species of python, growing to just over 60 centimetres. It is a placid species that rarely attempts to bite, even when handled. It occurs in the Pilbara and adjacent regions of Western Australia, not in Perth as the scientific name suggests. Depending on the substrate colour, the little snake ranges from brick red to yellowish brown. Though found in crevices on rocky outcrops, it is often associated with the large termite mounds that feature prominently in the arid landscape. It feeds on the geckos that also reside in these nests.

The **Large-blotched Python** or **Stimson's Python** (*Antaresia stimsoni*) grows to 90 centimetres. It is pale brown to yellowish brown with a contrasting pattern of dark transversely-elongate blotches. This widespread species is found in woodlands, rock outcrops, escarpments and caves from the west coast to Queensland and north-western New South Wales. Like other members of this group it has a fondness for caves and rock overhangs. It is sometimes encountered hanging from the roof or clinging to the walls at the entrance to a cave in order to strike at the small insect-eating bats that live in such caves as they emerge in the evening.

▲ Stimson's Python (*Antaresia stimsoni*). Longreach area, Qld. S. Wilson

◄ Children's Python (*Antaresia childreni*); eating a bat. Mitchell Falls, WA. J. Weigel

Pitless pythons: the Black-headed Python and Woma

▲ Black-headed Python (*Aspidites melanocephalus*). Moranbah area, Qld. S. Wilson

The two species of *Aspidites* are the only pythons in the world that do not have heat-sensitive pits. They also differ from most other pythons in having narrow heads that are not very distinct from the neck. These large, thickset species have banded bodies and reach around 2.5 metres long. Both prey heavily on reptiles that do not generate heat, so heat-seeking capabilities are of no advantage, yet they may opportunistically take mammals and birds when they encounter them. As well as constricting they use another method of subduing prey within the confines of burrows. This involves pressing the animal against the burrow wall with coils of the body and suffocating it.

Both are terrestrial and utilise abandoned burrows, soil cracks and hollow logs. They present impressive displays when harassed, compressing the neck and hissing with mouth partly agape, but they are generally reluctant to bite.

The **Black-headed Python** (*Aspidites melanocephalus*) has a glossy black head and neck in a striking contrast to the cream or light brown banded body. It occurs in dry areas of tropical northern Australia. It has been observed with just the black head and neck protruding from cover. This may be a technique to raise the snake's temperature without exposing the whole body.

▲ Woma (*Aspidites ramsayi*); showing black patch above eye. Condamine area, Qld. S. Wilson

The **Woma** (*Aspidites ramsayi*) ranges from pale yellow to reddish brown, with numerous irregular darker bands. Juveniles have a black blotch over each eye, a pattern that is retained by adults in eastern populations. It occurs across vast tracts of the arid west and interior, in habitats ranging from red sandhills and spinifex, to rocky areas, shrublands and dry woodlands. The south-western populations are severely threatened by land clearing and predation, and the eastern populations in New South Wales and Queensland have also suffered declines.

The Woma sometimes employs an unusual hunting method known as caudal-luring. The tail is positioned near the head and, when potential prey is observed nearby, it is wriggled to entice the animal within striking distance. It is not unusual for Womas to have the end of the tail missing, possibly a consequence of using the tail as bait. No doubt some animals actually seize and damage the tail tip before being killed themselves.

Woma (*Aspidites ramsayi*). Moomba, SA. S. Wilson

Plain big pythons: Water and Olive pythons

Most pythons sport conspicuous patterns but the two species in the genus *Liasis* have uniform colours without so much as a band or blotch between them. These pythons share large robust bodies, sleek, smooth scales and a long head distinct from the neck. Both are restricted to tropical northern Australia. They are terrestrial to semi-aquatic pythons that feed on mammals, birds and reptiles.

The 2.5 metre **Water Python** (*Liasis mackloti*) is olive brown to almost black, with a pronounced iridescence to the scales similar to the sheen of petrol on water. As its name suggests, this is Australia's most aquatic python. It is found mainly near freshwater creeks, lagoons, swamps, rivers and dams. Researchers studying a huge population of Water Pythons at Fogg Dam in the Northern Territory have shown them to be very adaptable. During the dry season they hunt water rats by locating them in the deep soil cracks. When the wet season arrives and the whole area is flooded, the pythons become aquatic and feed on water birds and their eggs.

The **Olive Python** (*Liasis olivaceus*) ranges in colour from yellow brown to olive brown, with a pearly sheen to the scales. There are two subspecies. *Liasis olivaceus olivaceus* occurs across northern Australia and grows to about 4.5 metres, while the Pilbara Olive Python (*Liasis olivaceus barroni*), from the Pilbara region of Western Australia, is reported to reach 6.5 metres. Though found in a wide variety of habitats, they are most often encountered along watercourses in rocky areas. They probably favour tight-fitting rock crevices and cavities as shelter sites and shaded waterside localities to ambush prey. Very large individuals consume mammals such as large wallabies. Sadly, Olive Pythons frequently fall victim to traffic on northern Australian roads, due in part to their length and their superficial resemblance to large venomous snakes.

▶ Olive Python (*Liasis olivaceus*). Lawn Hill, Qld. S. Wilson

▼ Water Python (*Liasis mackloti*). Iron Range, Qld. S. Wilson

Carpet snakes and their kin

▲ Rough-scaled Python (*Morelia carinata*).
Captive bred. S. Swanson

Between them, the five moderate to very large species of pythons of the genus *Morelia* cover most of the continent. They are mainly nocturnal but can often be encountered basking and sometimes foraging during the day. They are a diverse group with the head distinct from the neck. Some are almost completely arboreal while others are equally content on the ground, on rock faces or in trees. Included are the Australian Scrub Python, which is Australia's largest snake, the rare and unusual Rough-scaled Python, with its uniquely keeled scales, a mixed bag of Carpet Pythons, and the beautiful Green Python.

The **Rough-scaled Python** (*Morelia carinata*) is slender with keeled scales and a head that is very distinct from the neck. It is restricted to the northern Kimberley region of Western Australia, and was only discovered by Europeans in the 1970s. Since then only a small number of specimens have been observed in the wild but a captive breeding program has been extremely successful. It is mainly arboreal, living in sheltered monsoon forests within remote gorges. It has formidably long teeth, which are used to good effect with its distinctive threat display of gaping the mouth. These dagger-like teeth may have evolved to deal effectively with rock rats that can shed skin and fur when grasped. Why it has rough, keeled scales is unknown.

The **Australian Scrub Python** (*Morelia kinghorni*) is Australia's largest snake, reaching 6 metres, although there are unconfirmed reports of specimens attaining 8 metres. It is relatively slender, but large individuals are capable of eating wallabies and similarly sized mammals without too much trouble. Australian Scrub Pythons are common in the rainforests of north-eastern Queensland, but they also extend into a range of peripheral habitats.

The 4-metre **Oenpelli Python** (*Morelia oenpelliensis*) inhabits the rocky cliffs and gorges of the Arnhem Land Escarpment in the north-east of the Northern Territory. Countless generations of local Aboriginal people know this python, and against a

▲ Australian Scrub Python (*Morelia kinghorni*). Cairns area, Qld. S. Wilson

backdrop of rock faces richly daubed with their Dreamtime history and stories, the giant snakes lie in ambush for large mammals such as rock wallabies. This python was unknown to Europeans until the 1970s.

The **Green Python** (*Morelia viridis*) is almost completely arboreal. Adults are bright green while the juveniles are vivid yellow. It is widespread in New Guinea but in Australia is only found in the rainforests of the Iron and McIlwraith Ranges on Cape York in northern Queensland. The extraordinary shift from juvenile to adult

53

▲ Oenpelli Python (*Morelia oenpelliensis*); captive animal. G. Swan

colour can take place gradually over months, or abruptly in a matter of weeks. It is not associated with skin shedding. When at rest the Green Python adopts a distinctive looped coil on a branch or vine.

Juveniles generally live in foliage along clearings and forest edges. They hunt near the ground, where they wriggle their tails as lures to capture terrestrial skinks. Adults live higher in the forest and prey on mammals and birds. This python is a striking example of convergent evolution, being similar in colour, arboreal habits, resting posture and juvenile colour change, to the South American Emerald Tree Boa (*Corallus caninus*).

The most widespread and well-known Australian pythons are the various races of **Carpet Python** (*Morelia spilota*). There are seven extremely variable subspecies identifiable by locality, colour and even breeding behaviour. Whether all these are valid subspecies or merely colour variants remains to be seen, but between them they cover most of Australia. Many of them are found in or near urban areas, where they take up residence in roofs and play an important role as efficient, silent and biodegradable mouse traps.

The **Diamond Python** (*Morelia spilota spilota*) is the most southerly of all pythons, extending from coastal New South Wales into north-eastern Victoria. It is black with a yellow spot on each scale, and scattered clusters of dark-edged pale yellow blotches.

▲ Green Python (*Morelia viridis*); adult. Iron Range, Qld. S. Wilson

▲ Green Python (*Morelia viridis*); juvenile. Iron Range, Qld. S. Wilson

▲ Diamond Python (*Morelia spilota spilota*). Hawkesbury River, NSW. S. Wilson

It differs from other subspecies in the behaviour of courting males, who congregate around the same female during the mating season. In the other subspecies males are intolerant of each other at this time of year and engage in combat.

The **Western Carpet Python** (*Morelia spilota imbricata*) is found in the south-western region of Western Australia. It is brown to blackish brown with dark-edged pale blotches transversely elongated on the back, with a longitudinal stripe along the anterior flanks. It has been suggested that this race is declining in numbers due to urban spread, but this seems at odds with other subspecies that still occur in large numbers in similar urban environments.

The **Jungle Carpet Python** (*Morelia spilota cheynei*) has the smallest distribution of any of the carpet pythons, occurring in the tropical rainforests of the Atherton Tableland in Northern Queensland. In this region it tends to be found along the forested river courses. This subspecies is surrounded within its range by the Coastal Carpet Python (*Morelia spilota mcdowelli*) although there appears to be little intergradation between the two. Generally this python has a smaller average adult size than the other carpet pythons at 1.5 metres.

It is a variable form, usually with a very striking pattern of yellow bands, blotches or stripes against a blackish background.

▲ Western Carpet Python (*Morelia spilota imbricata*). Cowaramup, WA. R. Browne-Cooper

▲ Jungle Carpet Python (*Morelia spilota cheynei*). Innisfail, Qld. S. Wilson

A venomous Australian success story: elapid snakes

▲ Myall Snake (*Suta suta*); eating a mouse. Aramac, Qld. S. Wilson

Virtually all of Australia's venomous snakes belong to the family Elapidae. These front-fanged snakes include most of the famous names such as taipans, death adders, brown, black and tiger snakes. However, the majority are inoffensive, weakly venomous species that live out their lives unseen and unheard of by most Australians.

Elapids have a pair of hollow fangs. When they bite, venom is forced from a gland at the back of the head through the fangs into the victim. The primary use of venom is to help the snake to kill or immobilise prey. It also contains components that speed up the breakdown of food. Venom has a minor function as a defensive weapon against predators, as even the most lethal snakes rely first on escape and then on posturing and bluff before resorting to actually biting an animal many times larger than themselves.

There are more than 130 described species of Australian elapids. They are the largest and most diverse group of snakes in Australia, placing this continent in the unique situation of venomous snakes outnumbering non-venomous snakes.

We have our isolation to thank for this. Outside Australia, huge numbers of snakes in the family Colubridae dominate the snake fauna of all continents, but colubrids are relatively recent arrivals here, and are restricted to the tropical north and subtropical east. This has left a vast and richly diverse suite of habitats at the disposal of elapid snakes, which have

▲ Black-naped Snake (*Neelaps bimaculatus*); burrowing through soft sand. North-West Cape, WA. S. Wilson

evolved to occupy most of the various niches dominated by colubrids elsewhere.

Australia's elapids demonstrate how one family of snakes can exploit a wide range of resources, modifying their size, shape and venom toxicity in the process. They range from small, stout, boldly-banded burrowing snakes that wriggle through loose sand and soil cracks to slender, racy species as fast as greased lightning. There are fat, sluggish, viper-like elapids lying concealed under leaf litter and large, mobile, highly venomous elapids a metre or two long cruising open ground or lying coiled on riverbanks across the continent.

Some elapids have even made themselves at home in the sea. They have valvular, dorsally placed nostrils, laterally compressed bodies and paddle-shaped tails to propel them forward. These marine elapids – the sea snakes – live in all tropical seas except the Atlantic, but their centre of diversity is the Australian region. They live and breed in the sea and never voluntarily leave the water.

Elapids include both live-bearers and egg-layers. Species in cooler areas generally carry thin-shelled eggs within their bodies until the young are fully formed, 'hatch' and are then born live. This solves the problem of seeking sites with warm stable temperatures to incubate the embryos in cool climates. Live-bearers occur throughout Australia but most tropical species lay eggs.

Elapids eat vertebrates. There is no such thing as a vegetarian or omnivorous snake, and even as juveniles the Australian elapids are not known to habitually eat insects or other invertebrates. The larger species tend to have the broadest diets, opportunistically taking mammals, birds, reptiles, frogs and sometimes even fish. There are significant exceptions, as taipans prey exclusively on

▲ Narrow-banded Shovel-nosed Snake (*Brachyurophis fasciolatus*). Perth, WA. S. Wilson

mammals from birth, and have evolved an appropriate highly toxic venom to deal with prey capable of retaliating. As well as injecting venom some elapids wrap their prey in coils, using constriction to assist in subduing the animal.

Elapids hunt at different times and employ a variety of capture methods, but in spite of their diverse shapes and lifestyles they have largely focused their collective attention on a single abundant vertebrate resource. Most Australian elapids eat lizards. There are nearly 650 different kinds of lizards covering the entire continent. And most lizards, particularly skinks, are smooth-scaled, protein-packed and long-bodied for easy ingestion. There is nowhere better for a lizard specialist to live than Australia!

Nearly 80 per cent of the 97 terrestrial Australian elapids rely heavily on lizards as a major part of their diet, and almost half eat nothing but lizards from birth to adulthood. The large snakes with generalist diets start life by eating lizards before graduating to include more diverse prey. With so many species of snakes targeting the same food resource, it helps to partition their methodology – how they find and catch their food. Using stealth, speed and ambush, snakes have left few if any safe havens for their wary prey.

Several elapids have exceptional diets. Bandy-bandys eat only blind snakes of the family Typhlopidae, which they presumably locate beneath the soil using chemical cues collected on their forked tongues. A few species are frog specialists, while some shovel-nosed burrowing elapids feed largely or entirely on reptile eggs.

▲ Eastern Brown Snake (*Pseudonaja textilis*); juvenile eating a lizard. Brisbane, Qld. S. Wilson

▲ Ingram's Brown Snake (*Pseudonaja ingrami*). NT. S. Wilson

▲ Black-headed Sea Snake (*Hydrophis coggeri*). The valvular nostrils are positioned on the top of the snout. Ashmore Reef, WA. R. Grace.

▼ Black-headed Sea Snake (*Hydrophis coggeri*). Ashmore Reef, WA. R. Grace

THE ONES TO LOOK OUT FOR: DANGEROUS AUSTRALIAN SNAKES

Bites from any venomous snake, regardless of how small and inoffensive, should be treated as a POTENTIALLY SERIOUS threat, irrespective of whether any books (including this one) list the species as 'not dangerous'. Individual tolerances to even the mildest of venoms vary considerably. Weakly venomous species are known to have inflicted fatal and near-fatal bites.

Most Australian elapids have mild venom, and many are unwilling or unable to bite. But included among Australian snakes are some of the world's most lethal species.

For some snakes, there is a high probability of death or very serious harm from an untreated bite. But in all, fewer than 30 are considered to have bites that are potentially fatal. A number of these species occur only in remote areas, while others thrive on the edges of all Australian towns and cities. Admire them from a distance, for there is elegance in their fluid movements and beauty in their perfect structure. But leave them alone and they will happily do likewise.

▲ Highlands Copperhead (*Austrelaps ramsayi*). Mt Kosciuszko National Park, NSW. S. Wilson

Cool customers: the Copperheads

The three copperheads (*Austrelaps*) are moderate to large snakes with smooth, semi-glossy scales and barred lips. They are found in south-eastern Australia, including alpine regions, Tasmania and the Bass Strait islands. These are extremely cold-tolerant snakes and may come out from cover on cool, even overcast days when other reptiles are nowhere to be seen. Although diurnal, they become active at night during hot weather. Their main prey is frogs but they also eat lizards, other snakes and small mammals. They give birth to live young. Copperheads are secretive, inoffensive

▲ Highlands Copperhead (*Austrelaps ramsayi*); the lips are prominently barred. Ben Lomond, NSW. G. Swan

snakes. If threatened, their flattened necks, loud hisses and low sideways sweeps with the head and forebody are largely bluff. Though reluctant to bite, even when provoked, they are DANGEROUSLY VENOMOUS.

The **Highlands Copperhead** (*Austrelaps ramsayi*) is usually dark grey, reddish brown to blackish with prominent vertical bars on the lips. It occurs in the cool highlands from eastern Victoria to northern New South Wales, favouring moist areas associated with woodlands, forests and heaths. It is a stout-bodied snake, seldom reaching more than 1 metre. In some regions it is mistakenly called a 'Yellow-bellied Black Snake' due to the cream to yellow colouring along the lower flanks.

Telltale signs

→ Prominently or weakly barred lips.
→ Stocky build.
→ Occur in cool to cold regions.
→ Active at low temperatures.

▲ Highlands Copperhead (*Austrelaps ramsayi*); juvenile. Apsley Falls, NSW. G. Swan

▲ Lowlands Copperhead (*Austrelaps superbus*). Northdown Swamp, Tas. S. Wilson

▲ Lowlands Copperhead (*Austrelaps superbus*). Healesville, Vic. S. Wilson

▼ Pygmy Copperhead (*Austrelaps labialis*).
Cleland, SA. P. Mirtschin, Venom Supplies.

The **Lowlands Copperhead** (*Austrelaps superbus*) varies from reddish brown to dark grey with yellow to orange on the lower flanks and weakly barred lips. It occurs in Victoria, South Australia and Tasmania, including islands in Bass Strait where the largest individuals of up to 1.7 metres are found. It favours moist low-lying areas, usually in association with swamps, lagoons and watercourses, especially where dense tussock grasses grow. This is a common snake in some of Melbourne's outer eastern suburbs.

The **Pygmy Copperhead** (*Austrelaps labialis*) is smaller than other copperheads, reaching a maximum length of about 85 centimetres. It occurs in shades of brown to grey, sometimes with a darker vertebral stripe and a dark bar across the nape. The lips have prominent vertical bars. It is found on Kangaroo Island, South Australia, where it occupies a wide range of habitats, and a limited area of the Mount Lofty Ranges near Adelaide, where it appears restricted to high altitude stringybark forest.

Tiger in name but not in nature: Tiger snakes

The **Tiger Snake** (*Notechis scutatus*) is moderately robust with a broad, somewhat flattened head and smooth, weakly glossy scales. It is named because of the banded pattern of some individuals, but colouration is extremely variable, with unbanded snakes occurring in most populations. In much of South Australia and the Bass Strait islands, these snakes are often completely black.

Historically there have been two species of Tiger Snake recognised, divided into five subspecies. However, recent work indicates that there is only one highly variable species. It is widespread across eastern and southern Australia, including Tasmania and the Bass Strait islands.

Size is extremely variable, with the evolution of both gigantism and dwarfism on some island populations in response to the type of available prey. On Chappell Island in Bass Strait, dependence on a temporary glut of fat muttonbird chicks favours large sizes, commonly exceeding 1.5 metres. But on Roxby Island off Eyre Peninsula in South Australia, dwarfs less than 1 metre long subsist on small skinks.

On the mainland, with a diverse diet of frogs, lizards, birds and mammals, average maximum sizes lie between these extremes.

The Tiger Snake has an undeserved reputation as being very aggressive, yet it is quite a timid snake that avoids confrontation. Very large individuals are often quite unconcerned by the presence of people. Even when provoked they give plenty of warning with an impressive threat display, flattening the neck and forebody and hissing loudly. Only as a last resort will the snake strike, but given its abundance around southern cities it is not surprising that this highly venomous species is second only to the Eastern Brown Snake as the most common cause of snake-bite death in Australia.

Telltale signs

→ Generally near water or among tussock grasses.

→ Stout body, often banded.

→ Will flatten neck and forebody turning to present widest angle to threat.

▲ Tiger Snake (*Notechis scutatus*). Wollongong area, NSW. G. Swan

◀ Tiger Snake (*Notechis scutatus*). Coomalbidgup Swamp, WA. R. Browne-Cooper

▲ Tiger Snake (*Notechis scutatus*). Canungra, Qld. S. Wilson

▲ Tiger Snake (*Notechis scutatus*). Chappell Island, Tas. S. Wilson

▲ Tiger Snake (*Notechis scutatus*). Tas. S. Wilson

When black ain't black: the Black snakes

▲ Collett's Snake (*Pseudechis colletti*). Richmond area, Qld. S. Wilson

It seems curious that the seven species in the genus *Pseudechis* are widely known as the 'black snakes'. Just one is always black, a couple are brown, another has a yellow blotch on each scale, and yet another has cream to orange-pink markings. Their smooth scales range from weakly glossy to highly polished. These large snakes all exceed 1 metre and some commonly reach 2 metres or more. Most species are active by day and night depending on temperature. Because they occur throughout mainland Australia, there is a general trend towards nocturnal activity in the north and diurnal foraging in the south. When threatened they flatten the neck and forebody and hiss loudly, presenting the broadest aspect towards the perceived threat.

Black snakes eat a wide variety of vertebrates, including mammals, frogs, birds, reptiles and fish. Unfortunately they are highly susceptible to the poison of Cane Toads and populations of black snakes tend to crash when this introduced menace appears on the scene. In the Brisbane area there is evidence of a subsequent rise in Red-bellied Black Snake numbers as surviving generations probably avoid eating toads.

Most are egg-layers producing up to 19 eggs. The Red-bellied Black Snake gives birth to live young that are enclosed in a clear membrane from which they hatch within a few minutes of laying. All are regarded as DANGEROUSLY VENOMOUS.

Telltale signs

→ Robust body with smooth scales.
→ Broad head only slightly distinct from neck.
→ Will flatten neck and forebody, turning widest angle towards threat.

▲ Spotted Mulga Snake (*Pseudechis butleri*). Hell's Gate, WA. S. Wilson

▲ Mulga Snake (*Pseudechis australis*) Glenmorgan, Qld. S. Wilson

▲ Mulga Snake (*Pseudechis australis*). Sturt National Park, NSW. G. Swan

▲ Mulga Snake (*Pseudechis australis*); juvenile. Yathong Nature Reserve, NSW. G. Swan

▲ Red-bellied Black Snake (*Pseudechis porphyriacus*). Belrose, NSW. G. Swan

The **Mulga Snake** (*Pseudechis australis*), also known as the **King Brown Snake**, is poorly named, as the Mulga (*Acacia aneura*) forms only part of its vast distribution and individuals are not always brown. This extremely variable snake, ranging from yellowish brown or reddish brown to dark olive, has a reticulated pattern formed by dark-edged scales. It is the largest and most widespread species within the group, occurring across most of mainland Australia except the more humid eastern and southern regions. A large Mulga Snake putting on a defensive display is an impressive sight. While it is fairly placid and disinclined to bite, if it does so it chews while biting, injecting the greatest venom yield for any Australian snake.

The **Red-bellied Black Snake** (*Pseudechis porphyriacus*) is everybody's idea of the typical black snake. Its body is a sleek, glossy black with a red to cream belly and bright red lower flanks. The tip of the snout is brown. It usually lives close to waterways and moist areas where frogs are common. It is also fond of fish, including eels, when it can catch them. Unlike other black snakes the Red-bellied Black Snake is only active by day. Despite its reputation for being aggressive and highly dangerous, this elegant snake is inoffensive and reluctant to bite. Though it is rightly considered to be potentially dangerous, there are no proven human fatalities despite its occurrence along the populated eastern seaboard.

There is a widespread urban myth that if there are black snakes around you won't get brown snakes. They may eat the occasional brown snake but they generally prefer different habitats, with the black snake seeking moister areas.

▲ Red-bellied Black Snake (*Pseudechis porphyriacus*); defensive display. Brookfield, Qld. S. Wilson

▲ Spotted Black Snake (*Pseudechis guttatus*); black colour form.
Pillaga region, NSW. K. Griffiths

The variable **Spotted Black Snake** (*Pseudechis guttatus*) ranges from plain glossy black to individuals with scattered pale grey, cream to pink spots and flecks. It is also known as the Blue-bellied Black Snake because of the blue-grey ventral surface. While it inhabits a range of habitats in the eastern interior, including rocky slopes and woodlands, it is primarily a snake of low-lying flood-prone areas with heavy, cracking alluvial soils. Such fertile areas are ideal for a range of crops. Some populations remain common alongside agricultural development while others have severely declined.

▲ Spotted Black Snake (*Pseudechis guttatus*); cream colour form. Texas, Qld. S. Swanson

▲ Spotted Black Snake (*Pseudechis guttatus*); juvenile. Dubbo, NSW. G. Swan

When is a brown snake a 'Brown Snake'?

There are many brown-coloured snakes but not all of them are 'brown snakes'. The seven species of *Pseudonaja* are mostly large, highly venomous snakes and exhibit a bewildering range of colours, from light tan to almost black, with or without bands, spots or blotches. In all species the belly is usually flecked with orange. They are generally slender with a narrow head, large eyes and smooth, slightly glossy scales.

Brown snakes are found over most of mainland Australia, excluding Tasmania and the extreme south-east of Victoria. Many inland and northern areas support two or more species. They are diurnal or nocturnal depending on temperature, so in southern Australia they are often seen by day while in the tropics brown snakes tend to be more active at night. These are the snakes most likely to be encountered by people because they are relatively large, active species that have adapted extremely well to disturbed rural and urban environments.

Brown snakes have benefited from land clearing and the introduction of a new food resource in the form of the house mouse. They feed on a wide variety of vertebrate prey (including other snakes and even their own kind), subduing them with a combination of powerful venom and constriction. All are egg-layers.

Brown snakes have a reputation for being aggressive, yet radiotelemetric studies (following snakes with implanted transmitters) reveal them to be extremely secretive animals that spend most of their time inactive. When encountered they almost invariably flee and only become defensive when cornered and provoked. A rearing brown snake, following every move with mouth partly agape and orange-flecked belly clearly visible, is definitely something to be seriously avoided. But even this frightening stance is largely bluff, to be followed by real strikes only if provocation continues.

Brown snakes account for two-thirds of Australian snakebite fatalities. Excluding the small Ringed Brown Snake (*Pseudonaja modesta*), all are regarded as DANGEROUSLY VENOMOUS.

▼ Eastern Brown Snake (*Pseudonaja textilis*). Oakey, Qld. S. Wilson

Telltale signs

→ Juveniles of most species have a black blotch on the head and a band on the nape.

→ Flecked bellies.

→ Moderate to large snakes with slender bodies, narrow heads and large eyes.

→ Fast and alert.

▲ Eastern Brown Snake (*Pseudonaja textilis*). Nyngan, NSW. G. Swan

The **Eastern Brown Snake** or **Common Brown Snake** (*Pseudonaja textilis*) ranges from light grey-brown to black, but most adults are shades of brown. On very dark individuals, the orange ventral flecks are often grey. All young have a black blotch on the head and a black band across the nape. Most are otherwise unmarked but a proportion, even within one litter, may have numerous prominent, narrow black bands on the body. These usually disappear with age although bands are occasionally retained to adulthood. The inside of the mouth is pink. It occurs through the eastern half of Australia in most habitats except alpine regions. Favourite habitats are open woodlands, grasslands and partly cleared farmland featuring logs and haystacks. It is extremely alert and nervous, responding aggressively if provoked by raising the head and forebody into an S-shape.

◀ Eastern Brown Snake (*Pseudonaja textilis*); in defensive pose. Tilpa, NSW. G. Swan

▲ Eastern Brown Snake (*Pseudonaja textilis*); banded juvenile. Goulburn, NSW. G. Swan

▲ Eastern Brown Snake (*Pseudonaja textilis*); banded adult. Rosevale, Qld. S. Wilson

The **Western Brown Snake** or **Gwardar** (*Pseudonaja nuchalis*) occurs in dry habitats across mainland Australia, excluding parts of the east coast and southern areas. Across this vast area there is a confusing array of colour forms, with several completely different-looking snakes sometimes occurring in the same locality. It is probable that a number of species are included within this unwieldy complex. This snake has a large, distinctive strap-like scale on the front of the snout and the inside of the mouth is blue.

The **Dugite** (*Pseudonaja affinis*) occurs from southern Western Australia to far western South Australia. This variable snake ranges from shades of brown without pattern to densely speckled individuals. There are three subspecies; a large mainland form reaches 2 metres in length, and two dwarf populations on islands off the west and south coasts of Western Australia range in size from 85 centimetres to 1.2 metres. Their circumstances appear to parallel those of some Tiger Snake populations, where small prey such as lizards dictates the size of snakes isolated on islands, while the larger mainland populations can also prey on mammals.

◄ Western Brown Snake (*Pseudonaja nuchalis*); the scale on the front of the snout is large and strap-like. Hermidale, NSW. G. Swan

▲ Western Brown Snake (*Pseudonaja nuchalis*). Mutawintji National Park, NSW. G. Swan

▲ Western Brown Snake (*Pseudonaja nuchalis*). Bollon, Qld. S. Wilson

▼ Western Brown Snake (*Pseudonaja nuchalis*). Hungerford area, Qld. S. Wilson

▲ Western Brown Snake (*Pseudonaja nuchalis*). Hermidale, NSW. G. Swan

▲ Dugite (*Pseudonaja affinis affinis*). Hyden area, WA. S Wilson

▲ Dugite (*Pseudonaja affinis affinis*); eggs hatching. Sorrento, WA. S. Wilson

▲ Dugite (*Pseudonaja affinis exilis*). Rottnest Island, WA. S. Wilson

▲ Ringed Brown Snake (*Pseudonaja modesta*). Uluru, NT. S. Wilson

▲ Speckled Brown Snake (*Pseudonaja guttata*). Barkly region, NT. G. Swan

Taipans: the ultimate snakes?

▲ Coastal Taipan (*Oxyuranus scutellatus*). Cairns, Qld. S. Wilson

Stories about taipans (*Oxyuranus*) abound. Mention snakes in any northern Queensland pub and tales soon unfold of taipans outrunning men galloping on horseback, attacks without provocation, and even couplings with Carpet Snakes to produce super snakes with powerful venom and constriction. Taipans are actually secretive animals that invariably prefer retreat to confrontation. Many encounters are avoided simply because the snake has spotted a person approaching and slid away unseen. However, if provoked or cornered, taipans are nervous and aggressive, with a frightening capacity to deliver extremely lethal venom with a series of lightning-fast strikes.

There are three species of taipan, including one discovered in late 2006. So far only one Central Ranges Taipan (*Oxyuranus temporalis*) is known from a remote area near the borders of Western Australia, South Australia and the Northern Territory. It can only be assumed at this stage that its ecology is similar to other taipans.

Taipans are diurnal snakes with large eyes and long narrow heads. They are dietary specialists, preying exclusively on mammals, mainly rats. The two well-known species, the Coastal and Inland Taipans, employ a strike-and-release method to secure prey that has the capacity to retaliate when bitten. By striking fast, injecting a massive overdose of highly toxic venom, then immediately releasing the prey, the snake is able to follow the animal until it collapses and dies. For such a strategy to be

Telltale signs

→ Long narrow heads and large eyes.
→ Active during the day and quick to retreat.

▲ Coastal Taipan (*Oxyuranus scutellatus*). Cairns, Qld. S. Wilson

effective, the animals must perish quickly and be accessible.

Taipans are egg-layers. The newly hatched young of other large elapid snakes begin life on a diet of skinks, then graduate to larger prey. But for the specialised taipan, life begins with a litter of young mice.

Rightly or wrongly, some consider taipans as the pinnacle of snake evolution. They are large, swift, keenly aware of their surroundings and, according to those who have kept them, intelligent. All taipans are DANGEROUSLY VENOMOUS, and accurately regarded as among the world's most lethal snakes.

The **Coastal Taipan** (*Oxyuranus scutellatus*), also sometimes called the Eastern Taipan, grows to about 2 metres, with rare specimens known to reach over 3 metres. The long head is paler than the body, with a distinctly angular brow and orange-brown eyes. The scales are weakly keeled on the neck. Colour ranges from yellow-brown to almost black, with prominent orange blotches scattered over the cream belly.

Coastal Taipans occur in woodlands, sclerophyll forests and canefields from about Grafton on the north coast of New South Wales to the tip of Cape York. There are separate populations in the northern Kimberley region and the northern parts of the Northern Territory, and a New Guinea subspecies (*O. scutellatus canni*) on the far northern Torres Strait island of Saibai. Mammals as large as bandicoots have been recorded as prey items.

This is the most familiar and feared taipan because its eastern Australian distribution borders on many populated areas, particularly in tropical north

▲ Coastal Taipan (*Oxyuranus scutellatus*); juvenile feeding on a mouse. Mt Morgan, Qld. S. Wilson

Queensland. Before taipan-specific anti-venom was produced in 1955, death from a taipan bite was a near certainty.

The **Inland Taipan** (*Oxyuranus microlepidotus*), also known as the Western Taipan, Small-scaled Snake and Fierce Snake, grows to 2 metres. Colour depends on the season. In summer snakes are pale yellow-brown with dark-edged scales creating a herring-bone pattern, and the head and neck are glossy black. In winter they adopt much darker hues that tend to mask most of their pattern. The belly is cream to yellow with orange blotches. Both summer and winter colour forms resemble some variants of the Western Brown Snake, resulting in many misidentifications.

Inland Taipans are restricted to remote, largely featureless desert terrain centred on the Cooper Creek drainage system of inland Queensland and South Australia. The harsh habitat is characterised by blistering heat and years of drought, punctuated by rare rain events that transform the landscape. The fortunes of the snake are intimately linked with a local rodent called the Long-haired Rat (*Rattus villosissimus*). The snakes shelter in deep soil cracks and the burrows of the rats, and feed on the mammals almost exclusively. In a 'feast and famine' scenario, the rat populations explode during good seasons and crash when resources are depleted. Snake numbers rise and fall in response.

Despite the common name 'Fierce Snake', this shy species rarely attempts to bite. This is probably just as well, considering it possesses the most toxic snake venom known.

▲ Inland Taipan (*Oxyuranus microlepidotus*); winter colour form. Morney Plain, Qld. S. Wilson

▼ Inland Taipan (*Oxyuranus microlepidotus*); summer colour form. Morney Plain, Qld. K. Griffiths

Rough and ready: the Rough-scaled Snake

▲ Rough-scaled Snake (*Tropidechis carinatus*). Mt Glorious, Qld. S. Wilson

The **Rough-scaled Snake** *(Tropidechis carinatus)*, also known as the Clarence River Snake, grows to about 90 centimetres. Colour ranges from olive to brown with darker irregular bands or blotches across the body. The broad rectangular head is distinct from the neck and the non-glossy scales are strongly keeled, giving rise to the common name. It occurs in moist habitats such as rainforests, wet sclerophyll forests and creek margins from the central coast of New South Wales to the Fraser Island area of Queensland. A separate population occurs in the uplands of north-eastern Queensland.

The Rough-scaled Snake is semi-arboreal and may be encountered in quite dense vegetation several metres above the ground. While primarily nocturnal it can also be active during the day. It is a dietary generalist, preying on frogs, small mammals, birds and lizards.

This DANGEROUSLY VENOMOUS snake overlaps in some regions with the superficially similar, non-venomous Keelback or Freshwater Snake (see page 36). These are the only two snakes in eastern Australia that share prominently keeled body scales. They also share broadly similar colourations, being shades of brown with variable dark markings. On closer examination there are significant differences. The Rough-scaled Snake has a straight mouth and patternless upper lips while the Keelback has an upcurved mouth and dark sutures between the scales along the upper lips.

More definitive differences relate to scales under the tail. The Rough-scaled Snake has one row of undivided scales along the underside of the tail whereas the Keelback sports two rows of divided scales. There is also a tendency within their areas of overlap for Rough-scaled Snakes to occur at higher altitudes.

The Rough-scaled Snake is a nervous species that will quickly move away if disturbed. However it will defend itself vigorously and bite readily if cornered.

Telltale signs

→ Non-glossy, keeled scales.

→ Undivided scales beneath the tail.

→ Found in moist areas.

▲ Rough-scaled Snake (*Tropidechis carinatus*). Mt Glorious, Qld. S. Wilson

▼ Rough-scaled Snake (*Tropidechis carinatus*). Mt Glorious, Qld. S. Wilson

Living by stealth and ambush: Death Adders

▲ Common Death Adder (*Acanthophis antarcticus*); concealed in leaf litter. Mt Mee, Qld. S. Wilson

Australia is the only continent with no vipers, family Viperidae. In their absence, some elapid snakes of the genus *Acanthophis* have evolved to fill a similar niche. These sluggish, well-camouflaged and sedentary snakes lie concealed in leaf litter or under low shrubs and grasses. Important features of this group are a short, thick body, a broad head distinct from the neck and an abruptly slender tail.

Their similarity to vipers was not lost on early settlers, who were reminded of the Adder (*Vipera berus*) from Britain and Europe. They named the Australian snakes 'death adders' because of the high mortality from bites before anti-venom became available. The corruption 'deaf adders' may derive from their reluctance to move away when disturbed.

Death Adders are ambush predators that feed on a broad variety of vertebrates. The slender tail has a segmented tip and soft spine, and they lie with this resting near the head. When prey is detected, the snake wriggles the tail convulsively, mimicking a grub or worm to lure the animal within striking distance. Its ability to strike so suddenly and with such mind-boggling speed is unnerving to witness, particularly considering the snake is slow moving and prone to lie motionless for days on end. The strike is accurate and lethal, as powerful venom is injected deeply through long fangs.

Telltale signs

→ Short, thickset body, broad triangular head.
→ Slender tail with a flattened segmented tip, coloured black, white or yellow.
→ Usually motionless and reluctant to move when disturbed.

▲ Common Death Adder (*Acanthophis antarcticus*). Dajarra, Qld. S. Swanson

Common Blue-tongue Lizards (*Tiliqua scincoides*) are often mistaken for death adders because the thick-set, banded lizards look superficially similar as they move through grass or undergrowth. Sadly, this often has a tragic outcome for the Blue-tongue.

Death Adders have declined in many areas. They can be regarded as biological indicators of environmental quality as they appear extremely susceptible to degraded conditions. Weeds, altered fire regimes, introduced predators and toxic prey in the form of the introduced Cane Toad all play a part in the demise of these snakes from sites where they were once extremely common. At the best of times Death Adders can be difficult to see, though occasionally they move about on warm nights, particularly when males are searching for mates.

There are four widely recognised Australian species of Death Adders, though several distinct populations have been named and some of these may be valid species. Between them they cover most of mainland Australia except Victoria. All are live-bearers, with litters of over 30 young recorded.

The **Common Death Adder** (*Acanthophis antarcticus*) is usually less than 50 centimetres long, although giants of 1 metre have been recorded. Two colour forms occur, reddish brown and grey. Both have irregular paler bands across the body. The scales are smooth and non-glossy, and the head scales and those on the forepart of the body may be slightly ridged. It lives in a variety of habitats including semi-arid shrublands, heaths and rainforest edges in eastern and southern Australia. It is

▲ Common Death Adder (*Acanthophis antarcticus*); grey colour form. Figtree Stn, Qld. S. Wilson

▼ Common Death Adder (*Acanthophis antarcticus*); red colour form. Mt Mee, Qld. S. Wilson

absent from Tasmania and probably extinct in Victoria.

The **Desert Death Adder** (*Acanthophis pyrrhus*) is relatively more slender than the Common Death Adder, with strongly ridged scales on the head and body. It is rich red to pale reddish brown with narrow yellowish bands. When threatened it flattens its body, parting the scales to more sharply reveal these bands. It inhabits spinifex deserts and rocky hills in the western half of Australia.

Death Adders occurring among spinifex on stony soils in the Pilbara and North West Cape regions of Western Australia were recently confirmed as a distinct species, the **Pilbara Death Adder** (*Acanthophis wellsi*). This variable snake is related to the Desert Death Adder and the two species appear to hybridise where their ranges meet. The body is reddish brown with prominent bands, and some individuals have conspicuously black heads.

▲ Desert Death Adder (*Acanthophis pyrrhus*); the tail is positioned in front of the head as a lure. Carouse Dam Mine, WA. B. Maryan

▲ Desert Death Adder (*Acanthophis pyrrhus*). Port Hedland area, WA. S. Wilson

▲ Pilbara Death Adder (*Acanthophis wellsi*). Newman area, WA. B. Maryan

LIZARD-EATERS OF THE NIGHT: SMALL, NOCTURNAL ELAPIDS

In all but the coolest Australian habitats, a significant proportion of elapid snakes are small nocturnal species that prey mainly or entirely on lizards. Rather than evolving larger eyes to deal with lower light, the general trend among nocturnal elapids is to have relatively small eyes. In foraging at night, they rely less on eyesight and more on chemical cues to investigate cavities and other shelter sites where they locate and capture sleeping diurnal lizards. Nocturnal lizards are also encountered while active, and it is likely that other lizards are captured by day when they inadvertently blunder into a refuge harbouring a resident snake. Most of these snakes respond to threats by thrashing or rearing rather than relying on an ability to flee swiftly.

The Crowned snakes

▲ Golden-crowned Snake (*Cacophis squamulosus*); threat display. Mt Glorious, Qld. S. Wilson

The four species of Crowned Snakes (*Cacophis*) occur in woodlands and forests along the east coast of Australia from north-eastern Queensland to just south of Sydney. They are small to medium sized snakes with smooth shiny scales and distinctive pale collars or streaks on their necks. By day they shelter in damp sites under rocks, logs and leaf litter. When threatened these snakes

Telltale signs

→ Pale band around head.
→ Small eye.
→ Top of head darker than body.
→ Smooth shiny scales.

▲ White-crowned Snake (*Cacophis harriettae*). Deception Bay, Qld. S. Wilson

raise the head and forebody, and mock-strike with the mouth closed. Interestingly they strike with the snout lower than the crown of the head, presenting the dark top of the head bordered by the paler crown. It has been suggested this resembles the open mouth of a larger snake to a would-be predator. All are egg-layers. They are not considered dangerous.

The **White-crowned Snake** (*Cacophis harriettae*) grows to about 50 centimetres and is dark grey above and below. A pale band four or more scales wide extends across the nape and forward along the sides of the head. The top of the head is black. This snake is found in forests and heaths in northern New South Wales and eastern Queensland. It thrives in the modified landscape of Brisbane, living in gardens, compost heaps and among pot plants, and turning up at night on doorsteps in the heart of the city. It is considered one of the most common suburban snakes in that region.

▲ White-crowned Snake (*Cacophis harriettae*). Deception Bay, Qld. S. Wilson

The smallest crowned snake, the **Southern Dwarf Crowned Snake** (*Cacophis krefftii*), only reaches about 30 centimetres long. It is black to dark brown above and pale yellow below, with the ventral scales conspicuously dark-edged. The top of the head is dark, edged by a narrow pale band 1–2 scales wide. The Southern Dwarf Crowned Snake extends from the central coast of New South Wales to mid-eastern Queensland.

The **Golden-crowned Snake** (*Cacophis squamulosus*) is the largest species, reaching 65 centimetres long. It is dark brown to grey above and pink to orange below with a mid-ventral line of black spots. A fawn or brassy yellow streak sweeps along each side of the face, back onto the neck but does not join to form a complete band. Its impressive rearing stance has led one naturalist to affectionately refer to this species as the 'pocket cobra'. It is

distributed along the coast from Wollongong in New South Wales to mid-eastern Queensland. In the northern suburbs of Sydney it is frequently brought in at night by the household cat.

▲ Southern Dwarf Crowned Snake (*Cacophis krefftii*) Cooroy, Qld. S. Wilson

▲ Golden-crowned Snake (*Cacophis squamulosus*). Mt Glorious, Qld. S. Wilson

Golden-crowned Snake (*Cacophis squamulosus*); with its distinctive ventral pattern. Mt Glorious, Qld. S. Wilson

The Naped snakes and their kin

▲ Orange-naped Snake (*Furina ornata*); brightly banded nape. Wollombi Stn, Qld. S. Wilson

The five snakes in the genus *Furina* range from small, slender, brightly patterned species just 40 centimetres long to moderately robust, drably-marked snakes reaching nearly 1 metre. They have smooth, very glossy scales, slightly depressed heads and small black eyes. Some species have a red to yellowish brown band across the nape, although this may disappear as the snake ages. Between them they cover most seasonally dry or well-drained parts of mainland Australia, excluding the cooler southern regions. They feed almost exclusively on skinks, subdued by a combination of envenomation and constriction. They are egg-layers. All are terrestrial, sheltering under rocks or logs, among rotting wood, in disused termite mounds and soil cracks.

Some of these snakes are poorly known. Dunmall's Snake (*Furina dunmalli*) is listed as Vulnerable, having suffered extensive habitat loss with the clearing of vast tracts of Queensland's Brigalow Belt. The Yellow-naped Snake (*F. barnardi*), listed as Rare, is enigmatic and could feasibly be a variant of the widespread and common Orange-naped Snake (*F. ornata*). The two largest species, Dunmall's Snake and the Brown-headed

Telltale signs

→ Glossy smooth scales.

→ Small black eyes and slightly flattened head.

→ Nocturnal, usually found in dry areas.

→ Often a reddish band across the nape.

Snake (*F. tristis*) are pugnacious if provoked and could produce symptoms severe enough to require medical treatment. At the other end of the scale, the diminutive Red-naped Snake (*F. diadema*) is inoffensive and unlikely to bite, but if harassed will rear its head and mock-strike at its aggressor.

The **Orange-naped Snake** (*Furina ornata*) is the most widespread species, occurring across huge areas of northern and inland Australia. Although reaching 65 centimetres, it is not regarded as dangerous and is very reluctant to bite, although it will thrash and rear if threatened. The wide red or orange band separating the glossy black head and neck darkens as the snake gets older and may virtually disappear.

▲ Dunmall's Snake (*Furina dunmalli*). Glenmorgan, Qld. S. Wilson

▼ Red-naped Snake (*Furina diadema*). Myuna Stn, Qld. S. Wilson

▲ Orange-naped Snake (*Furina ornata*); weakly banded nape. Goods Island, Torres Strait, Qld. S. Wilson

The secretive snakes: Small-eyed Snake and kin

▲ Eastern Small-eyed Snake (*Cryptophis nigrescens*). Mt Crosby, Qld. S. Wilson

Five glossy, mainly patternless snakes of the genus *Cryptophis* (meaning 'secretive snakes') have small dark eyes, depressed heads and squarish snouts. They live in eastern and northern Australia. Only one species has any pattern – the Black-striped Snake (*C. nigrostriatus*) has a dark head and telltale stripe down the back. The group also includes the enigmatic Pink Snake (*C. incredibilis*), with the smallest known distribution of any Australian venomous snake. It is found only on Prince of Wales Island in southern Torres Strait.

All are normally encountered by day under debris or at night crossing roads. Females give birth to live young with up to 11 in a litter. One species has been involved in a number of extremely serious bites including a human fatality, so all should be regarded as POTENTIALLY DANGEROUS.

▲ Black-striped Snake (*Cryptophis nigrostriatus*). Moranbah area, Qld. S. Wilson

Telltale signs

→ Nocturnal and secretive.

→ Mostly patternless.

→ Glossy, smooth scales.

→ Squarish snout, very small to moderate black eyes.

The **Eastern Small-eyed Snake** (*Cryptophis nigrescens*) grows to about 50 centimetres although exceptional individuals up to 1 metre have been recorded. With its shiny black body, and pink to cream belly, it looks rather like a miniature Red-bellied Black Snake (see page 74). However, the pale ventral colour does not come up onto the lower flanks, while on the Red-bellied Black Snake the ventral pigment is most intense and conspicuous along the lower sides. In addition to lizards, the Eastern Small-eyed Snake is known to prey on frogs and other snakes, including its own kind.

It is the most widespread species, occupying a variety of habitats along the east coast and ranges from Victoria to north-eastern Queensland. It often shelters under flat rocks and other surface debris and also behind the loose bark on fallen or standing trees. Twenty-eight individuals have been found in the one shelter site during winter.

Serious bites have been recorded from this species.

Albino snakes are rarely found in the wild. The albino Eastern Small-eyed Snake pictured here is a dramatic contrast to the normal black individuals.

▲ Eastern Small-eyed Snake (*Cryptophis nigrescens*); albino. Kenilworth, Qld. S. Swanson

▼ Pink Snake (*Cryptophis incredibilis*). Prince of Wales Island, Torres Strait, Qld. S. Wilson

In the deep south-west: the Square-nosed Snake

▲ Square-nosed Snake (*Rhinoplocephalus bicolor*). Ocean Beach, Denmark, WA. S. Wilson

The 45 centimetre **Square-nosed Snake** (*Rhinoplocephalus bicolor*) is the only member of its genus. It has a broad squarish snout, small dark eyes and smooth glossy scales. Adults are dark brown to dark grey with orange sides and a pearly cream belly. Juveniles are pale bluish grey. It inhabits moist, low-lying areas in the lower south-western corner of Western Australia, dwelling mainly in abandoned stick-ant nests. Ants construct these mounds of fine, dry, clipped vegetation overlying and filling an excavation in soft sand. These structures are unique to the south-west of Western Australia and are prime real-estate for many animals, including small skinks that are eaten by the Square-nosed Snake. These snakes seldom if ever bite and are not regarded as dangerous.

Telltale signs

→ Squarish snout.

→ Orange along the side of the body.

→ Limited to south-western corner of Western Australia.

Thrashing about: the Curl snakes

▲ Myall Snake (*Suta suta*). Peery National Park, NSW. G. Swan

The four species of Curl snakes (*Suta*) range in size from about 50 to 75 centimetres. They have smooth, weakly glossed scales and normally conspicuous eyes with pale irises. Curl snakes inhabit mainly dry, open areas over much of mainland Australia, excluding parts of the east coast and southern regions. They derive their name from their defensive behaviour of thrashing about wildly, flattening the body and curling it into a tight coil to conceal the head.

Though Curl snakes prey mainly on lizards, the largest species capture other vertebrates including small mammals. They shelter during the day beneath ground debris, under rocks, or in abandoned burrows. All species are live-bearers. They bite readily and although not regarded as life-threatening, large individuals may cause considerable discomfort.

The 60 centimetre **Myall Snake** (*Suta suta*) is extremely widespread, occurring throughout eastern and central Australia with an outlying population in the far north-east of Western Australia. It is reddish brown to grey with a dark hood on the head and a dark-edged pale stripe from the snout through the eye. Over much of its wide range, this is the most common small nocturnal elapid snake, often uncovered beneath boards or seen crossing roads at night. Large individuals could deliver serious bites.

Telltale signs

→ Smooth, glossy scales.

→ Broad depressed heads, usually pale irises.

→ If disturbed will thrash about wildly.

▲ Myall Snake (*Suta suta*). Collinsville area, Qld. S. Wilson

▶ Rosen's Snake (*Suta fasciata*). Yardie Creek, WA. S. Wilson

▼ Little Spotted Snake (*Suta punctata*). Wyndham area, WA. S. Wilson

Wearing a black cap: the Hooded snakes

▲ Dwyer's Snake (*Parasuta dwyeri*). Yathong Nature Reserve, NSW. G. Swan

The six species of Hooded snakes (*Parasuta*), ranging in size from 40 to 60 centimetres, are named for the black hood on the head and nape. On some species the hood is unbroken over the top of the head, and in others it is broken or notched by a paler background colour. Apart from some dark edges to the smooth, weakly glossed scales, they are otherwise patternless, though the Black-backed Snake (*Parasuta nigriceps*) sports a dark mid-dorsal stripe. The eyes are relatively small and dark.

Though these secretive snakes are essentially lizard specialists, blind snakes are also recorded prey items. They are widespread across the southern half of Australia, mainly in dry or well-drained areas. At some localities Hooded snakes are commonly found beneath rock slabs or old rubbish. All species are live-bearers. They are generally considered weakly venomous and not dangerous, although bites from large individuals are likely to produce uncomfortable symptoms. Complications from a recent bite in Victoria led to a human fatality.

Telltale signs

→ Black hood on head and nape.

→ Plain brown to reddish brown body.

→ Glossy scales and small dark eyes.

→ Nocturnal and secretive.

▲ Dwyer's Snake (*Parasuta dwyeri*). Yathong Nature Reserve, NSW. G. Swan

The 60 centimetre **Dwyer's Snake** (*Parasuta dwyeri*) has an unbroken black hood on the head. It occurs in a variety of habitats from south-eastern Queensland to central Victoria. It has been found under rocks so well embedded one wonders how it managed to get there. With a flattened head it is obviously an accomplished burrower, well able to access narrow spaces.

The **Little Whip Snake** (*Parasuta flagellum*) has the black hood broken by a pale band across the snout between the nostril and eye. It is named because of a defensive habit common to the hooded snakes and to many other small nocturnal snakes, thrashing and flattening the body when disturbed. It is common in dry areas of south-eastern Australia, including outcrops and grassy plains on the western edge of Melbourne. This is the most cool-adapted of Australia's small nocturnal elapids, extending to parts of southern Victoria where all other snakes are diurnal. Several of these snakes may often be found together under suitable shelter.

The **Black-backed Snake** (*Parasuta nigriceps*) is easy to recognise by the distinctive pattern, featuring a prominent dark stripe down the middle of its brown back. The black hood is unbroken from snout to nape, where it joins the dark body stripe. This widespread species extends across southern Australia, between central Victoria and Western Australia. Its core habitat appears to be the dry mallee woodlands.

▲ Little Whip Snake (*Parasuta flagellum*). Sellick's Beach, SA. S. Wilson

◄ Little Whip Snake (*Parasuta flagellum*) Sellick's Beach, SA. S. Wilson

► Black-backed Snake (*Parasuta nigriceps*). Mt Karong, Vic. S. Wilson

109

Collared Whipsnake (*Demansia torquata*) Moranbah area, Qld. S. Wilson

DAYTIME PURSUIT: LIZARD-EATERS IN THE SUN

Diurnal elapids tend to be large-eyed, using vision as well as chemical cues. The species that hunt lizards have particularly keen eyesight and fast reflexes. They locate their quarry by telltale movement and catch them on the run after a rapid pursuit. Included within this group are some of Australia's fleetest snakes. If approached they are quick to flee, relying on their speed, rather than posturing and bluff, to escape danger. Some are so swift it is difficult to comprehend how they can reach such velocities with no limbs.

Greased lightning: the Whipsnakes

◀ Yellow-faced Whipsnake (*Demansia psammophis psammophis*). Kurwongbah, Qld. S. Wilson

ground, looking about them as they survey their surroundings and seek prey. All are egg-layers producing clutches of up to 10 eggs.

There are no known deaths attributed to Whipsnakes but large individuals should be regarded as POTENTIALLY DANGEROUS.

The racy Whipsnakes (*Demansia*) are aptly named as their bodies are slender and whip-like and they have long thin tails. There are 13 species across Australia, excluding only the most southerly parts of the continent. The eyes are very large and the body scales smooth and matt-textured. Most species have a distinctive facial pattern that includes a pale-edged, dark 'teardrop' or comma below and behind the eye and a thin dark line across the snout; many of the smaller species also have dark markings on the nape.

In a sense these are the 'greyhounds of the snake world', using their acute vision to locate lizards, and their speed to run them down and catch them. Some Whipsnakes move with the head and forebody off the

The **Yellow-faced Whipsnake** (*Demansia psammophis*) is the most widespread Whipsnake, occurring over much of western, southern and eastern Australia. It is recorded to reach 1 metre but rarely exceeds 75 centimetres. A conspicuous dark line curves across the across the snout, and a distinct pale-edged dark comma sweeps

Telltale signs

- → Smooth, non-shiny scales.
- → Most species have a pale rim around the eye and a dark comma shape below the eye.
- → Slender, with large eyes.
- → Active during the day and fast moving.

▲ Yellow-faced Whipsnake (*Demansia psammophis reticulata*). Eglinton, WA. B. Maryan

back beneath and behind the eye. The three subspecies include distinctive forms featuring various reticulated patterns of dark-edged scales, orange-copper flushes on the head, anterior body and tail, or two reddish brown streaks from the nape to forebody. It is the most frequently seen Whipsnake, as populations continue to thrive in some urban areas.

The two largest Whipsnakes are referred to as the Greater and Lesser Black Whipsnakes. Both exceed 1 metre and are restricted to woodlands of northern Australia. They differ from other Whipsnakes in having much weaker facial patterns, with no dark line across the front of the snout, just a broken white circle around the eye and sometimes a short dark comma beneath the eye. The **Lesser Black Whipsnake** (*Demansia vestigiata*) grows to about 1.2 metres. It is blackish to dark grey or dark brown and usually reddish brown towards the tail. There is a spotted pattern on the body formed by markings on each scale. The head is lighter, with or without darker blotches.

Demansia flagellatio was described as a new species in late 2007 This small, colourful whipsnake from north-western Queensland grows to just over 70 centimetres. It has generated some interest since it was named because it is so strikingly attractive. The olive-brown, reddish brown to blue body becomes dull

▲ Yellow-faced Whipsnake (*Demansia psammophis cuprieceps*). Newman area, WA. B. Maryan

▲ Lesser Black Whipsnake (*Demansia vestigiata*). Moranbah area, Qld. S. Wilson

▼ Lesser Black Whipsnake (*Demansia vestigiata*); lacks the distinctive comma, prominent in most other whipsnakes. Beerwah area, Qld. S. Wilson

▲ *Demansia flagellatio.* Lawn Hill, Qld. G. Schmida

▲ Downs Whipsnake (*Demansia rimicola*). Sturt National Park, NSW. G. Swan

▼ Downs Whipsnake (*Demansia rimicola*); showing the bright orange-red underside. Sturt National Park, NSW. G. Swan

to bright yellow on the tail, while the head is boldly banded with black and yellow. Nothing is known about this Whipsnake but considering its extremely slender body it is safe to assume that the elegant animal can move like greased lightning!

The **Downs Whipsnake** (*Demansia rimicola*) was also named in late 2007. It inhabits grasslands and shrublands on cracking clay soils across the interior of Australia. This grey to olive-brown snake has narrow dark and light stripes along the body, and usually a broad dark band across the nape, but this is often obscure in adults. The underside of the body is bright orange-red. It can sometimes be seen basking on road edges but if approached it vanishes swiftly into one of the deep cracks that characterise its vast open habitat.

White-lips, Crowns and Sedges

▲ White-lipped Snake (*Drysdalia coronoides*). Falls Creek, Vic. S. Wilson

In temperate areas across southern Australia, two genera of small snakes largely replace the Whipsnakes as diurnal skink-hunters. There are two species of *Elapognathus*, restricted to the south-west of Western Australia, while three *Drysdalia* species extend from semi-arid heaths along the eastern coastline of Western Australia to the south-east, including alpine areas and Tasmania. They overlap with Whipsnakes in parts of eastern New South Wales.

These moderately slender snakes are not as extreme in build as the Whipsnakes. They have smooth, matt-textured scales, large eyes with round pupils and range in size from 30 to 70 centimetres. Some have a prominent white stripe along the upper lip and/or a band across the neck, and all have yellow, orange or reddish bellies. They require access to sunshine and thick low vegetation, so favoured habitats include heaths, shrublands and open forests, sometimes around the edges of swamps. They are usually seen basking beside tracks or on tussock grasses, and are quick to vanish when approached. All are live-bearing. They are reluctant to bite and not regarded as dangerous.

Telltale signs

→ Smooth non-glossy scales.
→ Prominent white stripe along upper lip or band across neck.
→ Yellow, orange or pink belly.

▲ White-lipped Snake (*Drysdalia coronoides*). Dead Horse Gap, NSW. G. Swan

The **White-lipped Snake** (*Drysdalia coronoides*) is most likely Australia's most cold-adapted snake, occurring in regions out of bounds to most other snakes, including the summit of Mount Kosciuszko. Populations in northern New South Wales are restricted to upland areas while in the south, including Tasmania, it is found from sea level to alpine elevations. In Tasmania it is a very common sight, slipping quickly from view along the edges of most of the famous walking trails. Locals there refer to this species as a 'whipsnake'. White-lipped Snakes are named for the distinctive white streak from the snout along the upper lip to the neck.

The **Short-nosed Snake** (*Elapognathus minor*) inhabits heaths and sedges bordering swamps in the lower south-west of Western Australia. It is characterised by its short snout, oblique yellow streak on each side of the neck and yellow-orange belly with black edges to the ventral scales. It is rarely encountered, perhaps because of the dense vegetation it inhabits. Its close relative, the **Crowned Snake** (*E. coronatus*), occurs in the same areas but is much more frequently seen because it extends into a broader range of heath and forest-edge habitats. The Crowned Snake is readily identified by the black collar across its neck. In addition to skinks, it includes frogs in its diet.

▲ Crowned Snake (*Elapognathus coronatus*). Albany, WA. S. Wilson

◀ Short-nosed Snake (*Elapognathus minor*). Rocky Gully, WA. S. Wilson

▼ Short-nosed Snake (*Elapognathus minor*); ventral aspect. Albany area, WA. S. Wilson

DIG, PUSH OR SLIDE: THE BURROWING SNAKES

▲ Unbanded Shovel-nosed Snake (*Brachyurophis incinctus*); the snout is quite distinctive. Longreach, Qld. S. Wilson

There are five genera containing 20 named species of snakes that have evolved to burrow. They have small eyes and varying degrees of shovel-shaped snouts to push their way through soil. It is curious that these small, generally robust snakes, which spend most of their lives buried beneath the ground, are often brightly coloured and banded. Most also have dark heads and napes. Unrelated species of burrowing snakes in other parts of the world, most of them belonging to different families, often feature the same striking colouration. As the snakes move the bands merge, creating an illusion called 'flicker-fusion' that renders the snake difficult to see. We are not certain why such colouration should be particularly associated with burrowing species, rather than other generally terrestrial snakes.

Most eat skinks but some specialise in finding and eating reptile eggs. The soft-shelled egg is punctured by enlarged teeth, and then swallowed, and the collapsed shell is passed through the gut. None are considered dangerous and many have never been known to bite a person. They are all egg-layers.

Telltale signs

→ Small snakes (less than 50 centimetres) with very shiny smooth bodies.

→ Dark bands on head and nape and small eyes.

→ Often bright bands or rings.

→ Snout often protruding, sometimes with a transverse cutting edge.

On its own

Antairoserpens warro is the only member of its genus. This secretive, little-known snake from north-eastern Queensland grows to only 37 centimetres. It is moderately robust with smooth glossy scales and a weakly shovel-shaped snout. It is yellowish to red-brown with each scale dark-edged, creating a bold reticulated body pattern. It occurs in tropical woodlands and open forests and probably feeds exclusively on small lizards.

▲ *Antairoserpens warro.* Rundle Range, Qld. S. Wilson

Shovel-nosed Snakes

▲ Australian Coral Snake (*Brachyurophis australis*). Riverside Stn, Qld. S. Wilson

The seven species of *Brachyurophis* are relatively robust burrowing snakes, collectively known as Shovel-nosed Snakes because their snouts feature a weak to acute transverse cutting edge. Most of these 30–40 centimetre snakes have bands across the body but their bellies are unmarked. All have broad dark bands across the head and nape. Between them they are widespread in dry habitats across mainland Australia except for the far south-western and south-eastern corners. While some members of this group eat small lizards, all probably take reptile eggs and several appear to be egg specialists.

The harmless **Australian Coral Snake** (*Brachyurophis australis*) is named for its coral pink colour and not for any similarity to its highly venomous namesakes, the coral snakes of North and South America. It is attractively patterned with numerous irregular bands formed by dark-edged pale scales. It is widespread in dry habitats across the eastern interior.

The **Southern Shovel-nosed Snake** (*Brachyurophis semifasciatus*) is a reptile egg specialist. It has been suggested that the ridge across the snout may help the shovel-nosed snakes lever individual eggs from an adherent mass as well as assisting passage through soil.

▲ Australian Coral Snake (*Brachyurophis australis*); head. Glenmorgan, Qld. S.Wilson

▼ Unbanded Shovel-nosed Snake (*Brachyurophis incinctus*). Longreach, Qld. S. Wilson

▼ Southern Shovel-nosed Snake (*Brachyurophis semifasciatus*). Cundeelee, WA. B. Maryan

The smallest burrowers

▲ Black-striped Burrowing Snake (*Neelaps calonotos*). City Beach, WA. S. Wilson

The two species of *Neelaps* are very slender snakes with a maximum length of 45 centimetres. They have narrow, flattened heads and protruding snouts with no cutting edges. Both occur in the south-west of Western Australia, inhabiting dry areas with loose sand. They prey upon small skinks, particularly the sliders of the genus *Lerista*. These snakes stalk the lizards below the surface of the sand before seizing and eating them.

The **Black-striped Burrowing Snake** (*Neelaps calonotos*), one of the most colourful Australian snakes, is also the smallest venomous species, reaching just 28 centimetres. Most individuals sport a distinctive black stripe enclosing a row of white spots down the middle of the back. It is found in dunes and sand plains with heath or banksia woodland. Because the entire distribution is restricted to a narrow coastal strip north and south of Perth, the snake is of conservation concern.

Ringed burrowers

▲ Jan's Banded Snake (*Simoselaps bertholdi*). Port Germein, SA. S. Wilson

The four species of *Simoselaps* are small, thick-set snakes with flattened heads and protruding snouts without sharp cutting edges. Three of the four species have conspicuous rings encircling the body. All are pale yellow to bright orange with black blotches on the head and nape. They shelter in loose sand or litter under trees and shrubs in dry to arid regions of western and central Australia. All are lizard specialists, employing weak venom and constriction to subdue burrowing slider skinks of the genus *Lerista*.

Jan's Banded Snake (*Simoselaps bertholdi*) is the best-known species, extending across arid southern Australia to the suburbs of Perth. On sunny winter days this 30-centimetre snake can be found just below the surface of exposed sun-warmed sand. In hotter weather it retreats to more sheltered sites under thick leaf litter. It differs from the closely related **West Coast Banded Snake** (*S. littoralis*) in having a broader black nape and dark edges to its yellow scales.

▲ West Coast Banded Snake (*Simoselaps littoralis*). Tamala Homestead, WA. S. Wilson

▶ Desert Banded Snake (*Simoselaps anomalus*); with a black head. Lake Mackay WA. B. Maryan

▼ Desert Banded Snake (*Simoselaps anomalus*); burrowing. Near Port Hedland, WA. B. Maryan

Bandy-bandys

▲ Eastern Bandy-bandy (*Vermicella annulata*) Ku-Ring-Gai National Park, NSW. G. Swan

The secretive bandy-bandys (*Vermicella*) can be locally common but are not often encountered due to their burrowing, nocturnal lifestyle. There are five species although only one, the Eastern Bandy-bandy (*Vermicella annulata*), is widespread, occurring over much of the eastern half of mainland Australia. It is the largest species, reaching 75 centimetres, but most adults are about 50 centimetres. Others have restricted distributions in northern, central and western Australia. As a group they are readily identifiable by the alternate black and white rings around the body, but the species are distinguished from each other by the number and width of those rings, and aspects of scalation.

Bandy-bandys feed exclusively on blind snakes of the family Typhlopidae and are capable of swallowing individuals as large as themselves. They are egg-layers and from 2 to 13 eggs have been recorded in a clutch. They are normally encountered on the surface during warm nights after rain. Bandy-bandys are not considered dangerous and indeed it seems almost impossible to get one to bite at all. When threatened they thrash and raise their bodies to form vertically-oriented loops.

Telltale signs

→ Very distinctive black and white rings around body.

▲ Eastern Bandy-bandy (*Vermicella annulata*); defensive pose. Mt Nebo, Qld. S. Wilson

▼ Eastern Bandy-bandy (*Vermicella annulata*); eating a blind snake. St Ives, NSW. G. Swan

THE FROG-EATERS: ORNAMENTAL SNAKES AND MUD ADDERS

▲ Ornamental Snake (*Denisonia maculata*). Moranbah area, Qld. S. Wilson

Two fat, sluggish snakes in the genus *Denisonia* have broad flat heads and prominently barred lips. Both are medium-sized snakes growing to around 40–50 centimetres. They have large eyes with pale irises and smooth, weakly glossed body scales. They are associated with deep soil cracks in low-lying flood-prone areas of eastern Australia.

These nocturnal snakes are among the few Australian species that feed almost entirely on frogs. The frogs are captured above ground by foraging snakes, and are probably taken by day when encountered below ground in soil cracks. Both species can be locally abundant in suitable habitats.

Because of their robust bodies and sedentary habits, they are often confused with death adders. If provoked, they flatten the body, thrash about and strike repeatedly. A bite from either species should be treated as POTENTIALLY DANGEROUS.

Telltale signs

→ Stout snakes with dark patch on head and barred lips.

→ Nocturnal, favouring low-lying areas.

The **Ornamental Snake** (*Denisonia maculata*) is restricted to drainage systems of mid-eastern Queensland where it shelters

▲ Ornamental Snake (*Denisonia maculata*). Myuna Stn, Qld. S. Wilson

▶ De Vis Banded Snake (*Denisonia devisi*). The Gums, Qld. S. Wilson

▼ De Vis Banded Snake (*Denisonia devisi*). Glenmorgan, Qld. S. Wilson

in the deep cracks in clay-based soil. These cracks also shelter the frogs that the snake feeds on. Studies during pipeline excavation reveal extremely high population densities in suitable habitat. More than 20 snakes were removed from a 1-kilometre transect of trench near Moranbah, Queensland. When the soil or topography change, numbers drop sharply – from abundant to absent over a few hundred metres.

De Vis Banded Snake (*Denisonia devisi*) is called the Mud Adder in some regions because it is stocky, banded and commonly found in damp areas. It occurs in the southern interior of Queensland and adjacent inland New South Wales. Researchers recently discovered a new, isolated population after following up reported sightings of 'death adders' near the Murray River in north-western Victoria.

SOGGY CUSTOMERS: MARSH AND GREY SNAKES

The two species of *Hemiaspis* are unusual in that these close relatives are markedly different in behaviour. One is a primarily diurnal species preying on skinks and frogs, the other is a nocturnal snake specialising in frogs. They are small snakes, reaching 60 to 70 centimetres long, with large eyes and smooth, matt to slightly glossy scales. Both are VENOMOUS, and bites from large individuals may cause marked local symptoms.

▲ Grey Snake (*Hemiaspis damelii*). Bendidee State Forest, Qld. S. Wilson

Telltale signs

→ Matt or slightly glossy scales.

→ Unpatterned bodies but distinctive head markings.

▲ Marsh Snake (*Hemiaspis signata*). Brisbane, Qld. S. Wilson

◄ Marsh Snake (*Hemiaspis signata*). Chaelundi State Forest, NSW. G. Swan

The **Marsh Snake** (*Hemiaspis signata*) is olive-brown to dark grey or black, with a distinctive pair of narrow pale stripes on either side of the head. The belly is dark grey or black, giving rise to another common name, the Black-bellied Swamp Snake. It lives in moist habitats beside creeks and in forests along the east coast and ranges from south-eastern New South Wales to south-eastern Queensland, with isolated populations in mid-eastern and north-eastern Queensland. Small Australian elapid snakes do not normally have broad diets but this snake is comfortable feeding on both skinks and frogs. It is diurnal, but during hot weather also becomes active at night.

The **Grey Snake** (*Hemiaspis damelii*) is a uniform greyish brown with a darker hood on the head. It occurs further inland, occupying woodlands and grasslands, particularly on flood-prone cracking soils, from the south-eastern interior of Queensland to the north-eastern interior of New South Wales. An outlying population lives on the Lachlan River of southern New South Wales. It is nocturnal, emerging from soil cracks to hunt frogs.

LOFTY ELAPIDS: THE ARBOREAL BROAD-HEADED SNAKES

▲ Broad-headed Snake (*Hoplocephalus bungaroides*); in defensive pose. Yalwal Plateau, NSW. S. Wilson

Australian elapid snakes are poor climbers. While many species, including brown and black snakes, have occasionally been recorded in trees and rafters, this is generally considered unusual, atypical behaviour. But the three species of Broad-headed Snakes (*Hoplocephalus*) are skilful and habitual climbers, aided by a lateral keel or notch on each belly scale. This allows them to grip bark and rock surfaces. They are found in forested areas, woodlands and outcrops along eastern Australia from just south of Sydney to north-eastern Queensland.

All are vertebrate feeders but with differing prey preferences. They are live-bearers, with females giving birth only every second year or even less frequently.

When threatened these snakes, named for their broad depressed heads, adopt a distinctive defence stance, striking repeatedly with the neck held in a tight S-shape and the head flattened. They are aggressive if provoked. There are no recorded deaths, but there have been severe reactions from bites so they must be considered POTENTIALLY DANGEROUS.

Telltale signs

→ Broad, flat heads.

→ Belly scales keeled along outer edges.

→ Distinctive head and body patterns.

The **Pale-headed Snake** (*Hoplocephalus bitorquatus*) reaches 80 centimetres. It is grey to almost black with angular black spots on the head, a distinct white or pale grey band on the nape and prominently barred lips. This is the most widely distributed of the Broad-headed Snakes, occurring in woodlands and open forests from the coast and interior of north-eastern New South Wales to north-eastern Queensland. It lives mainly near water, on large trees bearing hollows and loose bark. Favourite trees include ironbarks and river red-gums. At night it forages on the trunks, branches, and on the ground for its favourite prey, tree frogs, although lizards and small mammals are also taken.

The 90-centimetre **Broad-headed Snake** (*Hoplocephalus bungaroides*) is black with numerous yellow scales forming irregular bands. On occasions this striking colouration has led to confusion with small Diamond Pythons, with potentially dire results. This snake has an extremely

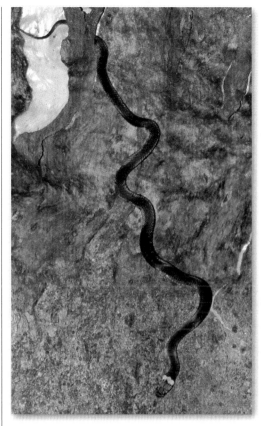

▲ Pale-headed Snake (*Hoplocephalus bitorquatus*); descending a tree. Gwabegar area, NSW. K. Griffiths

▲ Pale-headed Snake (*Hoplocephalus bitorquatus*); striking. Moranbah area, Qld. S. Wilson

Pale-headed Snake (*Hoplocephalus bitorquatus*); in tree crevice. Oakey, Qld. S. Swanson

restricted distribution, occurring only in the sandstone escarpments and outcrops between Sydney and the Nowra area. For most of the year, this primarily nocturnal snake shelters beneath exfoliating sandstone slabs, in windblown caves and in crevices. During warmer months it occupies hollow limbs in nearby eucalypts. Unfortunately the sandstone slabs it depends on have been indiscriminately removed for garden landscaping, causing numbers to decline dramatically, and restricting the snake to inaccessible ledges and cliff tops. It feeds mainly on the geckos and skinks that share its rocky habitat.

The largest of the broad-headed snakes is **Stephens' Banded Snake** (*Hoplocephalus stephensii*) which reaches 1.2 metres. Most specimens are brown with broad irregular blackish bands, although some individuals are unbanded. The lips are conspicuously barred even on otherwise patternless individuals. It occurs in wet and dry forests and rock outcrops from the central coast of New South Wales to south-eastern Queensland. Stephen's Banded Snake is arboreal, favouring large mature trees with hollows or extensive vine cover. Where it occurs on sandstone and granite outcrops it shelters under slabs and in crevices, climbing with ease over rock faces. It has a broad diet of vertebrates, taking lizards, small mammals, birds and frogs.

▲ Stephens' Banded Snake (*Hoplocephalus stephensii*). Mt Glorious, Qld. S. Wilson

▲ Broad-headed Snake (*Hoplocephalus bungaroides*); the broad, flattened head is quite distinctive. Yalwal Plateau, NSW. S. Wilson

133

ODDBALL OUT WEST: THE LAKE CRONIN SNAKE

▲ Lake Cronin Snake (*Paroplocephalus atriceps*). Middle Ironcap, WA. B. Maryan

The 60-centimetres **Lake Cronin Snake** (*Paroplocephalus atriceps*) is known from fewer than 10 specimens within a localised area in the semi-arid southern interior of Western Australia. This slender snake has large eyes with pale irises, smooth, brown, matt-textured scales and a very broad black head. Its closest relatives are probably the arboreal Broad-headed snakes of eastern Australia. Not a great deal is known about this snake except that it eats lizards and is nocturnal. Most of its habitat consists of dry woodlands and it may be arboreal, utilising loose bark and hollow limbs. With a single exception, all specimens have been collected on the ground at night, mostly crossing roads. Just one was found under a rock slab on one of the significant outcrops in the area. The use of trees and rocks accords with the site-selection of Broad-headed snakes. One recorded bite produced severe symptoms, so it should be regarded as DANGEROUSLY VENOMOUS.

▲ Lake Cronin Snake (*Paroplocephalus atriceps*). Lake Cronin, WA. S. Wilson

Telltale signs

→ Broad black head and large eyes.

→ Smooth non-glossy scales.

→ Restricted distribution.

IS IT AN ADDER? THE BARDICK

▲ Bardick (*Echiopsis curta*). Mount Lesueur, WA. B. Maryan

The **Bardick** (*Echiopsis curta*) is a short, stocky snake with a wide head distinct from the neck, and smooth matt-textured scales. Because of these features it somewhat resembles a Death Adder but lacks the lure on the tail-tip and bands across the body. Most are a uniform red-brown to grey but some individuals have white flecks on the sides of the head and neck, particularly in eastern populations.

Three isolated populations occur across southern Australia: the south-west of Western Australia; the Eyre Peninsula in South Australia; and from south-eastern South Australia to adjacent areas of Victoria and New South Wales. The Bardick occupies heathlands and mallee/spinifex habitats where it shelters beneath low shrubs or in spinifex clumps.

The Bardick is mainly nocturnal but can sometimes be seen basking during the day. Like the Death Adders it is slow-moving and is often encountered lying motionless among low shrubs. It has a broad diet, feeding on lizards, frogs and small mammals. It is pugnacious if provoked, striking and flattening the body. The bite should be regarded as POTENTIALLY DANGEROUS.

Telltale signs

→ Very stocky and adder-like.
→ Non-shiny scales and uniform colour.

▲ Bardick (*Echiopsis curta*). Big Desert, Vic. G. Swan

▲ Bardick (*Echiopsis curta*). Bunkers Bay, WA. S. Wilson

DOING IT SWIMMINGLY:
THE SEA SNAKES

▲ Horned Sea Snake (*Acalyptophis peronii*); foraging with head down a goby hole. Ashmore Reef, WA. R. Grace.

Elapid snakes are so versatile some have abandoned land and taken up residence in the sea. The sea snakes are so highly modified they have often been classified as a separate family but we now recognise them as marine elapids, closely linked to the Australian terrestrial elapids. About 33 species are known from Australian waters, most of them occurring in other areas of the Pacific and Indian Oceans.

There are two groups of marine snakes. The true sea snakes are born in the water, live their entire lives in an aquatic environment, and never voluntarily come onto land. Australia is a centre of diversity for this group. The other group, the sea kraits, feed in the sea but lay eggs and shelter on land. They are abundant in tropical regions to our north, east and west, but only strays venture into Australian waters.

Both groups of sea snakes have evolved specialised physical characteristics to cope with their demanding marine lifestyle. These include a laterally flattened paddle-shaped tail and valvular nostrils situated on top of the snout. The true sea snakes are the most highly modified. While their terrestrial cousins have broad ventral scales that span the width of the belly to aid locomotion, many sea snakes have greatly reduced the size of their ventral scales. This means their laterally-flattened bodies are superb for swimming but they are unable to move effectively on land.

Telltale signs

→ Totally aquatic but may be found washed ashore.
→ Laterally flattened, paddle-shaped tail.

Olive Sea Snake (*Aipysurus laevis*); often encountered by divers. Ashmore Reef, WA. R. Grace

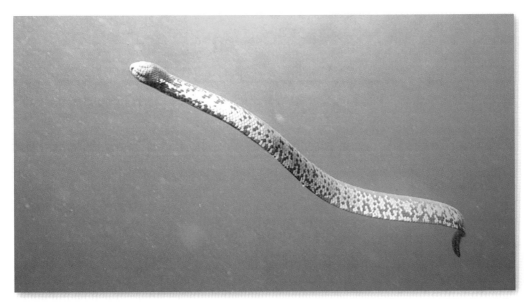

▲ Olive Sea Snake (*Aipysurus laevis*). Ashmore Reef, WA. R. Grace

Sea snakes are air-breathing and come to the surface to take breaths, but can remain submerged for several hours. At least one species has light-sensitive skin on the tail. This warns the snake, if it is sheltering in a cavity or under a ledge, when the tail is not concealed. Presumably, if the tail is hidden, the rest of the snake is too.

Most sea snakes utilise coastal and reef environments in tropical and subtropical regions, remaining close to the substrates as they forage or rest. Several forage in the shallow water on intertidal flats, but the Yellow-bellied Sea Snake is the exception. It is pelagic and occurs in deep ocean regions far from land.

Sea snakes eat fish and many can opportunistically prey on a wide variety of species. Several are eel specialists with highly modified body shapes that enable them to probe narrow holes and crevices. At least two sea snakes eat only fish eggs, and in the process have lost effective use of their fangs. They are the only sea snakes that can truly be considered harmless.

Most sea snakes are DANGEROUSLY VENOMOUS and all should be treated with the utmost caution. Bites are rare and usually caused when the snake is handled, but these snakes are sometimes inquisitive and may approach divers. Individuals found on beaches have been cast up by waves after storms and are generally helpless but still capable of delivering a serious bite.

The **Olive Sea Snake** (*Aipysurus laevis*) is a large and bulky snake that generally reaches nearly 2 metres, although larger individuals have been recorded. This extremely variable species ranges from purplish brown, with or without numerous cream-spotted scales, to golden brown or paler with or without scattered darker scales. The belly scales, about three times as broad as the adjacent body scales, are keeled with a small posterior notch.

This is one of the sea snakes likely to be encountered by divers. It can be locally abundant on reefs around northern Australia, New Guinea and the Coral Sea.

While normally found at depths of 5–20 metres, it has been sighted at 130 metres. Olive Sea Snakes forage by day and night, taking nocturnal fish during the day and diurnal fish at night.

The 1 metre **Yellow-bellied Sea Snake** (*Pelamis platurus*) is conspicuously marked, with sharply-delineated black above and yellow below; the tail is yellow with black spots. The belly scales are usually divided and only slightly broader than the adjacent body scales.

This is the only truly pelagic sea snake, ranging from the Cape region of South Africa through the Pacific and Indian oceans to the west coast of the Americas. Although normally occurring in warmer waters, individuals have been found on the Tasmanian, New Zealand and Siberian coasts. These are strays and most encounters involve snakes washed onto beaches after heavy seas.

Yellow-bellied Sea Snakes often aggregate where ocean currents converge. They feed on a wide variety of fish attracted to these slicks, seizing their prey with a sideways lunge of the head, or by suddenly swimming backwards to take unaware the fish swimming behind in their shadow. These snakes are largely avoided by predatory mammals, fish and birds. Experiments have shown that would-be predators will not take them even if hungry. Their colour possibly serves as a warning that they are toxic or unpalatable.

▲ Olive Sea Snake (*Aipysurus laevis*); mating pair. Ashmore Reef, WA. R. Grace.

▲ Yellow-bellied Sea Snake (*Pelamis platurus*). Mandurah, WA. R. Browne-Cooper

▲ Stokes' Sea Snake (*Astrotia stokesi*); with diver. Ashmore Reef, WA. R. Grace

The 1.5–2 metre **Stokes' Sea Snake** (*Astrotia stokesii*) is the bulkiest of the sea snakes with a very large head and thick neck. Colour ranges from creamy white to dark brown, and the pattern, pronounced on juveniles and usually obscure to absent on large adults, features large dark blotches alternating with narrow bars. The belly scales, about the same size as the adjacent body scales, are divided and strongly overlapping to form a very distinctive keel. This widespread snake extends through South-east Asia to the South China Sea and India, and occurs along the coast and coral reefs of northern Australia with strays turning up in more southerly regions during late summer.

An unusual aggregation of these snakes was reported in 1932 in the Malacca Straits. This was some 100 km long and 3 metres wide, comprising literally millions of snakes. The reason they congregated in such a manner is unknown.

The 2 metre **Elegant Sea Snake** (*Hydrophis elegans*) belongs to a group of sea snakes with extraordinary proportions. It has a small indistinct head, slender forebody and very robust, laterally compressed hindbody.

▲ Elegant Sea Snake (*Hydrophis elegans*). Bundaberg, Qld. S Swanson

▼ Stokes' Sea Snake (*Astrotia stokesi*). Darwin Harbour, NT. P. Horner

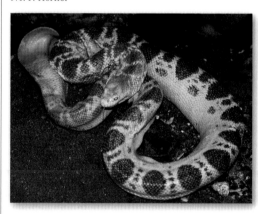

Juveniles are pale brown with a black head and numerous prominent broad dark bands, widest dorsally and ventrally, and often alternating with narrower bands. Adults are paler with a weaker pattern. The belly scales are slightly wider than the adjacent body scales. This widespread and abundant species occurs in deeper waters off northern Australia and southern New Guinea.

It feeds almost exclusively on eels, and the slender neck and forebody enable the snake to easily penetrate the narrow burrows of its prey.

Suggested reading

Bennett, R., 1997. *Reptiles and Frogs of the Australian Capital Territory*. National Parks Association of the ACT Inc, Canberra.

Bush, B., Maryan, B., Browne-Cooper, R. & Robinson, D., 2007. *Reptiles and Frogs in the Bush: Southwestern Australia.* University of WA Press, Nedlands.

Cogger, H.G., 2000. *Reptiles and Amphibians of Australia*. Reed New Holland, Sydney.

Coventry, A.J. & Robertson, P., 1991. *The Snakes of Victoria: A Guide to their Identification.* Department of Conservation & Environment, Melbourne.

Ehmann, H., 1992. *Encyclopedia of Australian Animals: Reptiles*. Collins Angus & Robertson, Sydney.

Greer, A.E., 1997. *The Biology and Evolution of Australian Snakes.* Surrey Beatty & Sons, Chipping Norton, New South Wales.

Griffiths, K., 2006. *Frogs and Reptiles of the Sydney Region*. Reed New Holland, Sydney.

Heatwole, H., 1999. *Sea Snakes.* Australian Natural History Series. UNSW Press, Sydney.

Hutchinson, M., Swain, R., & Driessen, M., 2001. *Snakes and Lizards of Tasmania.* University of Tasmania, Hobart.

Shine, R., 1991. *Australian Snakes: A Natural History.* Reed New Holland, Sydney.

Storr, G.M., Smith, L.A. & Johnstone, R.E., 2002. *Snakes of Western Australia.* Western Australian Museum, Perth.

Swan, G., 2007. *Green Guide: Snakes and Other Reptiles of Australia*. Reed New Holland, Sydney.

Swan, G., Shea, G. & Sadlier, R., 2004. *A Field Guide to Reptiles of New South Wales*. Reed New Holland, Sydney.

Swan, M. & Watherow, S., 2005. *Snakes, Lizards and Frogs of the Victorian Mallee.* CSIRO Publishing.

Swanson, S., 2007. *Field Guide to Australian Reptiles.* Steve Parish Publishing, Queensland.

Weigel, J., 1990. *Australian Reptile Park's Guide to Snakes of South-east Australia*. Weigel Photoscript, Gosford.

Wilson, S., 2005. *A Field Guide to Reptiles of Queensland*. Reed New Holland, Sydney.

Wilson, S., 2008. *Reptiles of the Southern Brigalow Belt*. World Wildlife Fund, Australia.

Wilson, S. & Knowles, D., 1988. *Australia's Reptiles: A Photographic Reference to the Terrestrial Reptiles of Australia*. Collins, Sydney.

Wilson, S. & Swan, G., 2008. *A Complete Guide to Reptiles of Australia*. Reed New Holland, Sydney.

More information

If you want to find out more about snakes and meet people with a similar interest, contact one of the organisations listed below. More details can be found at **www.reptilesdownunder.com**

ACT Herpetological Association, PO Box 160, Jamison Centre ACT 2614, margaretning@iprimus.com.au

Monaro Amphibian & Reptile Keepers, 16 Alfred Hill Drive, Melba ACT 2615, ssambars@bigpond.net.au

Australian Herpetological Society, PO Box R79, Royal Exchange, Sydney NSW 2000, mattmccloskey@msn.com

Hawkesbury Herpetological Society, PO Box 30, Emerton NSW 2770, hawkesburyherps@bigpond.com

Illawarra Reptile Society, PO Box 183, Albion Park NSW 2527, Zweers2@optusnet.com.au

Inverell Herpetological Society, 45 Chester Street, Inverell NSW 2360, info@invherpsoc.com

MacArthur Herpetological Society, Locked Bag 2, Narellan NSW 2567, Snake2snake@yahoo.com

New England Herpetological Society, 2/26 Anne Street, Tamworth NSW 2340, information@herps.org.au

North Coast Herpetology Group, 25 Arkana Avenue, Cundletown NSW 2430, thenchg@yahoo.com.au

Riverina Frog & Reptile Society, PO Box 712, Wagga Wagga NSW 2650, secretary@riverinafrogandreptilesociety.org.au

Shoalhaven Reptile Club, PO Box 890, Nowra NSW 2541, pkjorgo@aapt.net.au

Society of Frogs & Reptiles, PO Box 30, Jesmond NSW 2299, sofar@hunterlink.net.au

The Herpetological Society of Queensland, PO Box 322, Archerfield Qld 4108, herpsoc@hotmail.com

North Queensland Herpetological Society, PO Box 1180, Thuringowa Central Qld 4817, nqhs@snakenurse.com.au

South Australian Herpetology Group, c/- SA Museum, North Terrace, Adelaide SA 5000, vanweenen.Jason@saugov.sa.gov.au

Tasmanian Herpetological Society, 8 Clarke Street, Weymouth Tas 7252, ian.norton@qvmag.tas.gov.au

Tasmanian Reptile & Fauna Club, 38 Lovett Street, Ulverstone Tas 7315, thows@austarnet.com.au

The N. W. Coast Herpetological & Creepy Crawlies Club, 99 Winduss Road, Gunns Plains Tas 7315, lawnmower1@bigpond.com.au

Victorian Association of Amateur Herpetologists, 8 Fellmongers Road, Breakwater Vic 3219, vaah@geelong.hotkey.net.au

Victorian Herpetological Society, PO Box 4208, Ringwood Vic 3134, vhs@optusnet.com.au

Acknowledgements

Gerry Swan and Steve Wilson wish to thank Rob Browne-Cooper, John Cann, Roger Grace, Ken Griffiths, Paul Horner, Brad Maryan, Peter Mirtschin (Venom Supplies), Gunther Schmida, Geoff Swan and Steve Swanson for the use of their splendid images. We acknowledge the time, effort and finances they have spent on scouring the country for their subjects.

Gerry would like to thank his family, and in particular his wife Marlene, for their tolerance and sometimes amusement at the stream of strange herpetological specimens (human and otherwise) that keep appearing. He would also thank the people at New Holland, in particular Diane Jardine, who so competently organised schedules around our ever-changing comings and goings.

Steve would like to thank his wife Marilyn for her support and encouragement, and for indulging his compulsive obsession with reptiles. The writing was on the wall when a large portion of the honeymoon was spent hunting Greek vipers. He also thanks Mike Swan, Dave Knowles, Rod Hobson and Robert Ashdown for sharing their passion for herpetology, photography and quality time in the bush. Kieran Aland has allowed access to animals in his care for photography. Steve's parents, Joy and Ken, put up with more than most parents should, encouraging their son's interest while a procession of reptiles including dangerous snakes were smuggled into the family home.

Index

Also available from New Holland Publishers

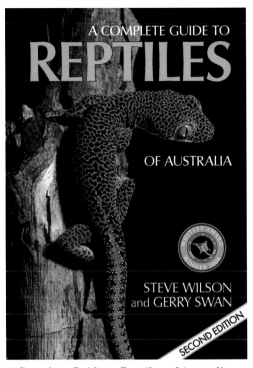

A Complete Guide to Reptiles of Australia
ISBN: 9781877069468

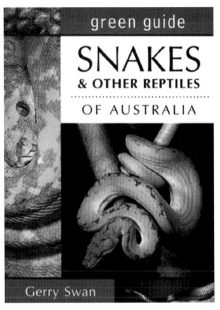

Green Guide: Snakes & Other Reptiles
ISBN: 9781864363425

A Field Guide to Reptiles of NSW
ISBN: 9781877069062

A Field Guide to Reptiles of Queensland
ISBN: 9781876334970

About the authors

Gerry Swan was born in Wellington, New Zealand, where there are no snakes, so his early interest in reptiles was focused on lizards. After moving to Australia in the 1960s, his interest was rekindled.

He is an Associate of the Australian Museum and past editor of the journal *Herpetofauna*, and works as a reptile consultant and author. He has written a number of books on reptiles including co-authoring with Steve Wilson *A Complete Guide to Reptiles of Australia*.

Gerry has a particular interest in the reptiles of the arid and semi-arid regions of New South Wales.

Steve Wilson has worked at the Queensland Museum for the past 20 years, educating the public, identifying specimens and sharing his passion for conserving Australia's unique biological heritage. His lifelong love affair with reptiles has taken him to some of Australia's most remote places and for the past 30 years he has been working to compile a comprehensive photographic documentation of Australia's reptiles.